LATIN LOVERS

DO WE REALLY EXIST?

The truth about Latin Lovers
revealed in true stories from the heart
and life of a passionate Latino.

PABLO G. CASTANEDA R.

Note for Librarians: A cataloguing record for this book is available from Library and Archives Canada at www.collectionscanada.ca/amicus/index-e.html
ISBN 1-4120-5080-4

PUBLISHING™

Offices in Canada, USA, Ireland and UK
This book was published *on-demand* in cooperation with Trafford Publishing. On-demand publishing is a unique process and service of making a book available for retail sale to the public taking advantage of on-demand manufacturing and Internet marketing. On-demand publishing includes promotions, retail sales, manufacturing, order fulfilment, accounting and collecting royalties on behalf of the author.

Book sales for North America and international:
Trafford Publishing, 6E–2333 Government St.,
Victoria, BC v8t 4p4 CANADA
phone 250 383 6864 (toll-free 1 888 232 4444)
fax 250 383 6804; email to orders@trafford.com
Book sales in Europe:
Trafford Publishing (uk) Ltd., Enterprise House, Wistaston Road Business Centre,
Wistaston Road, Crewe, Cheshire cw2 7rp UNITED KINGDOM
phone 01270 251 396 (local rate 0845 230 9601)
facsimile 01270 254 983; orders.uk@trafford.com
Order online at:
trafford.com/04-2888

10 9 8 7 6 5 4

ACKNOWLEDGEMENTS

God, thank you for giving me your love and mercy.

Jesus, thank you for being in my heart.

Papi and *Mami*, thank you for your support through all these years. You guys are great! *"LOS QUIERO MUCHO."*

Claudio and Annelie, thank you for being part of my life.

Lori, you are such a blessing in my life, thank you for your support. *"TE QUIERO MUCHO BEBA."*

Angie, thank you for believing in me and being a real friend through this new experience.

Monique, you rock girl!

Gabriela and Johanna, thanks for contributing imagination and style to this project.

Lily, thanks for making the right decision on the cover.

David, thanks for letting me buy your laptop and being such a great friend and example.

Summer Loves:
"They are shooting stars, an spectacular moment of
light in the heavens, a fleeting glimpse of eternity. In a flash
they're gone". (Nicholas Sparks).
"The Notebook"

"And I believe shooting stars last forever in the heavens"
(Pablo Castaneda).
"I built the house in my heart"

FORWARD

As I traveled to different countries around the world, "Latin Lover" was the label most often given to me. The label itself didn't bother me, it was the stigma attached to it. It was the stigma that provoked me to question, "What is a Latin Lover?" and "Do we really exist?" It was the stigma that sent me on a quest for answers. And it's the stigma that I desperately want to change.

Please allow me to tell my story. I want to redefine the term "Latin Lover." I want to share my life with you in hopes that you will have a greater understanding and a deeper appreciation for the true Latin Lover. I'd also like to share some of the valuable lessons God has taught me along the way. Each experience carries a piece of my heart and shows what God has done in my life. Writing makes me feel closer to God and allows me to better express who I am.

> I want to redefine the term "Latin Lover."

This book has been yet another adventure in my life. It's enabled me to re-experience many milestones and see them from a greater perspective and as they say, hindsight is 20/20. It's my hope that through this book, you will become more familiar with my culture and the source of my life's love and passion.

TABLE OF CONTENTS

WORD TO THE READERS

Through the exciting adventure of writing this book, I woke up many nights wondering if it was all just a dream. It was hard for me to believe that I was sharing my heart with you. This book has opened a countless number of doors in my heart and in my life. It's given me greater insight into my very soul. It's helped me to sort out the things in my past and has given me a healthier perspective on my future. I have new hopes, new dreams, and a renewed strength. Best of all, throughout this process God has given me new wisdom.

Through it all, I've wondered about you. Every time I sat down to pour out my heart, you were in the back of my mind. I wonder who you are, if you're a girl in college or a housewife struggling to hold a family together. Maybe you're a single mom trying to make ends meet, a grandma longing for the good old days, or even a guy striving to learn to love and care for women in a greater way. I wonder how you would define Latin Lovers right now and if that definition will change after you finish reading my story. I wonder what enticed you to pick up this book and I wonder even more if you'll put it down before you've read the last page. I wonder about your hopes, your dreams, and your fears and if you'll somehow find comfort within these few pages.

I have so many expectations for you and our time together. It's the deepest cry of my heart to tear down any misconception you may have about Latin Lovers and the Latin culture in general. More than that, I pray that your heart is touched through the simplicity of these thoughts. My most precious goal is that after you read this book you will have gleaned some small truth that you can apply to your life.

Chapter 1

Sharing With You

The typical stereotype of Latin men is that they are passionate worshippers of love who only use women to get what they want. But for me, love and passion are emotions that extend into every area of life, not just intimate relationships. Women expect me to be "Rico-suave," like the song, simply because I'm a Latino. They think I'm focused only on sexual gratification, and they don't realize that I have values, hopes, dreams, and a whole other life outside of relationships with women. Since I'm a Latino who loves, I'm termed a "Latin Lover" and I'm automatically stamped with all the negative connotations that go along with that title.

> The typical stereotype of Latin men is that they are passionate worshippers of love who only use women to get what they want.

Love and passion are the essence of who I am. This is something that I desperately want to convey so that people will have a greater understanding of my heart and who I am. I am, by nature, a passionate person. It's a passion that's powerful, real, and easy to get lost in. It's a passion for God, people, nature, family, my country, beauty, and creativity, as well as for the woman I choose to love. Everyday I try to have a greater understanding and get a

1

better grasp on the privilege of being a Latino. I try to figure out what is most important to me as a man: my goals, hopes, dreams, and things I want to accomplish in life. In light of these things, I simply could not rest knowing that most of the world has a distorted view of Latin Lovers. I felt obligated to do something, so I set out to redefine the Latin Lover.

To begin my quest, I asked various female friends from the United States and Europe to share their definitions of a Latin Lover. Here are some of their responses:

OPINIONS SHARED

"I think 'Rico-suave' type, dark skin, dark hair, smokey eyes, and somewhat of a man of mystery. But he also knows every move in the book." (Kelly)

"A Latin Lover is: Ricky Martin, Rico suave, night-life loving, hip swaying, disco dancing, open-shirt-ed, hairy-chested, slick, seductive guy that is a total charmer and not to be trusted." (Betsy)

"The term Latin Lover makes me think of a man who knows what to say, when to say it, and how to flatter... but doesn't mean what he says. He knows how to make a woman feel good. I don't think he's **only** try-ing to get her into bed, but he likes to have her 'eating out of his hand' or thinking that he's the most won-derful man on earth because he looks the right way and he says and does all the right things." (Angie)

"Antonio Banderas, now he's a Latin Lover. Of course, the first thing that comes to mind when someone says Latin Lover is someone who's very sexy, but I think that it's much more than that. He has to be dark, charming (to everyone, not just beautiful women), sincere, a beautiful dancer, and a true gentleman. I think that a Latin Lover has an appreciation for the finer things in life, but knows what is really important (the bohemian ideals of freedom, beauty, truth, and above all – love) which gives him a carefree attitude. He isn't necessarily the most handsome man you've ever met, but he has self-confidence." (Leah)

"When I think of a Latin Lover, I think sexual thoughts, romance, and hot summer nights on the beach with waves coming up." (Jennifer)

"A Latin Lover is a mythical romance novel character, the housewife affair dream guy, mostly based upon looks and sex appeal – tall, dark, young, and muscular. He doesn't say much because of a language barrier. He's not ideal for a long-term relationship. He's just a fling to make a woman feel desirable." (Joannah)

"A Latin Lover is a tan to dark man with dark hair a little on the long side and dark eyes that seem bottomless. He's masculine and confident with a smoldering sensuality that lies just below the surface. Personally I think men and women, Latin or not, can have these qualities. It seems to have more to do with how they feel about themselves than where they are from, although some cultures are much more in tune with their bodies and their sexuality than others." (Melanie)

"When I think of a Latin Lover, I think of affairs, weekend escapades, sex on the beach, and one night stands rather than long-term relationships. I imagine myself feeling more open, self-expressive, and adventurous with a Latino." (Michelle)

"A Latin Lover symbolizes someone who is hot in bed and knows all the right things to say and do to a woman to get her in bed and to keep her there. He has a reputation of being a sleazy, insincere sex addict. In Europe, having a Latin Lover implies lots of sexy, good things, but comes with it a hint of infidelity and style above substance." (Zoe)

According to the majority of these women, a Latin Lover is void of feelings and uses women only to satisfy himself. Most women think he's a Rico-suave, a mysterious, yet charming man who only lives for night-life, parties, and dancing. He's a man who never means what he says and his only goal in life is to get women into bed. He's the housewife-affair type, with a great sex appeal, who is definitely **not** ideal for a long-term relationship. He's simply a fling who makes women feel desirable and apparently women have nothing but sexual thoughts about him. Basically, what I learned from this inquiry was that women associate Latin Lovers with infidelity and sex. Opinions I received indicated that heated passion and the sexual experience are the only drives for Latin Lovers while feelings and long-term commitment are of no value. In hearing this, I felt ill and I didn't want to hear anymore. Up to this point I had only had transient encounters with this grotesque stereotype. Now I caught a glimpse of the full picture of the world's shallow understanding of Latin Lovers.

I believe that many of these opinions come from the stereotype that has been portrayed in the media. A "Latin Lover," according to the media, is a hot Latin singer who has all the sexy looks and "hip-shaking" moves.

One of the first Latinos portrayed by the media was Don Juan de Marco. He was charming and could make a woman's heart melt with his deep, sexy look. His love life was one conquest after another and he had thousands of stories to brag about.

Another Latin singer, Gerardo, coined the term "Rico-suave" with one of his greatest hits. The image he portrayed was undoubtedly responsible for the stereotype we know today. He flaunted his sculpted body and was never caught wearing a shirt. His long, dark, wavy hair was held back by a bandana. His dance was sensual and seductive, and he was always surrounded by women. Rico-suave became a popular song and inundated the media, leaving behind a wake of inaccuracy which now surrounds the Latin culture as a whole. Unfortunately, most women believe this shallow image of Latin Lovers.

The movie **ZORRO** hit the big screen with a redeeming portrayal of the Latin Lover. His heroic character dedicated his entire life to helping people. He fought for justice and he respected and valued women. He was handsome, charming, and confident. He didn't waste his time chasing after love because he knew that it would walk into his life at just the perfect moment. Though he could have easily managed it, his goal in life was **not** to have thousands of women. His mysterious ways, his values, and his beliefs touched the hearts of nearly everyone. Zorro taught us the importance of fighting for justice and a better way of life for those in need. In the end, he found true love, got married, and had a son. The boy grew up hearing stories about his father's great adventures. The story closes with Zorro imparting his love and passion for a life of serving others to his son. Zorro's life was not based on using love to conquer women, but on making the world a better place. He loved his family and had a mutual respect for all people. I'd like to think that this is a more accurate representation of Latin Lovers.

> Latinos are passionate, it's true.

I would like to defend myself by showing you that there is more to a Latino than the media's shallow stereotype would lead you to believe. But, at the same time I have to admit, that some of the stereotypes about Latinos have a basis in reality. For instance, Latinos are passionate people. Unfortunately, most people only stress the sexual aspect, and they don't recognize that this passion extends into **every** aspect of life. Latinos are also great dancers. Somehow, it's assumed that if you're good at dancing and moving your hips, then you must also be good in bed. Though based in reality, these slight twists result in a very perverted image of the truth. Perhaps the greatest mistake Latinos have made is one of passive silence. We've done nothing to change this stereotype. We've made no effort to share what we're really all about.

I love people and I share the most valuable thing I have with them, my heart. I don't even consider one-night stands or "flings," because that lifestyle neglects what is most important. I appreciate women and I'm faithful to the one I'm with. I value her life, her love, her goals, and her dreams. My aim is to complement her life, reciprocate her love, help her reach her goals, and make her dreams a reality.

I believe that only God can make me a real man, worthy of giving and receiving love. I would like to share my feelings on life, family, work, women, and how my relationship with God makes me complete. I want to share what I've learned in life so far, particularly what I've learned from women and why they're such a special part of my life. I want to share why family is important to me and why I want to be prepared for the day that I become a husband and a father. I want to share how the love relationships I've had have blessed me and given me a more humble, caring heart. I want to share how God has used the experiences in my life to show me how to live with love and passion. A love and passion that extend far beyond love relationships, into virtually every area of my life. I want to share my heart so that you may be able to understand me and the heritage I'm so proud to be a part of. I'm not sharing these things because I think I have life all figured out or because my philosophy on relationships is flawless. I'm sharing my life and my heart with you because I want to redefine the Latin Lover. I want to show the world that the typical stereotype of the Latin Lover is grossly wrong.

CHAPTER 2

THE IMPORTANCE OF FAMILY

B efore I delve into my life, I think I should give you my family background, information from my younger years, and explain a few of the things I've learned with that beautiful blessing of hindsight. It's difficult to know where to start describing the importance of my dear family, considering I could easily write volumes about them, so I'll start with my immediate family.

MY IMMEDIATE FAMILY

Papi (my father), Ernesto Castaneda Bailey, was born in Guatemala City on May 24, 1930. He came from a poor family of six and decided at a very young age that he was not going to let that poverty determine his fate. He resolved in his heart to create a better life. When he had a family, he would not allow them to suffer the same poverty he experienced. At age seven, as soon as he was big enough to shine shoes, he started working. When he was big enough for more physical labor, he got a job as a janitor. And finally, when his technical abilities caught up with his physical abilities, he was trained as an electrician. He wasn't necessarily the smartest in his field, but his determination, drive, and exceptional work ethic earned him an administrative position. Whatever he did, he worked at it with all his might.

Mami (my mother), Marina Rodriguez de Castaneda, lovingly called *La Mary* by the entire family, was born in Guatemala City on February 4, 1934. She came from a middle-class family of seven, she was a great student, and she loved to go to parties. She found a job she loved right out of high school. She worked as a secretary at a lumber yard. Though she only worked there for five years before becoming a full-time wife and mother, she came away with more than five years of experience and growth.

I'll never forget my parent's love story as I've heard them joyfully recount it a countless number of times. Cupid launched his first arrow the first time they laid eyes on each other at a soccer game on December 1, 1956. My father played on a team with my mother's older brother, who introduced them after the game. The encounter was brief, but between my mother's beauty and my father's charm, a second meeting was inevitable. This meeting took place a few weeks later at a Christmas party. They say, my mom often played hard to get, but my dad's steely determination applied to more than just his work and his pursuit of my mom was relentless. Cupid helped him complete his task that night when he asked my mom to dance. He was a great dancer and that's all it took. They danced for the entire night and he swept her off her feet. She agreed to go out with him and they dated for over a year before they became *novios* (boyfriend and girlfriend). They were married the following year on April 11, 1958. That day marked the beginning of a great adventure for the two of them. They started to become a great team and slowly their lives and personalities began to intertwine. My dad used to have a bad temper, but with God's help and the companionship of my loving mother, his life was changed and his heart was softened.

Their first son, Israel, was born on January 29, 1959. They say he was an angel and the first blessing they shared. He was a beautiful, curly headed blond with a smile that could light up any room. A few days before his third birthday, my parents were robbed at gun point. In the process, Israel ran into the street and was hit by a car. His tragic death nearly ended my parent's marriage, each one blaming the other. Not only did they blame each other, they blamed God. It was the most difficult time they've ever had to face, but by the grace of God, they were able to overcome their bitterness and anger toward one another and their heavenly Father. In hindsight, they say that the devastating loss and the difficult time that followed caused them to trust God in a greater way and develop a stronger love and marriage.

On August 14, 1962, my sister, Dina Annelie, was born. She was the balsam for their broken hearts and a blessing that served to reunite their marriage. She was exactly what they needed. My brother, Claudio, came almost two years later on June 12, 1964. The family was getting stronger and they felt God was helping them to become better parents. They were learning to forgive and their love was growing deeper. My dad bought a large piece of land and they moved into a nice home. His dream of providing a safe place for his children to play was finally a reality. My sister and brother had a great early childhood. They lived in a nice neighborhood and had a lot of friends. Many of the friendships that they built growing up are still alive and well today. The next door neighbors were such close friends that we even had a door put in connecting our two homes. The closeness of our two families is largely attributed to the huge earthquake that devastated Guatemala on February 4, 1976. Many people lost their lives and the entire country was in a state of shock. I had come on the scene unexpectedly, on January 30, 1975, more than a decade after my brother and sister. I had only recently celebrated my first birthday so I have no recollection of the earthquake or the aftermath.

Our house was completely destroyed by the quake. My family recalls what a difficult time it was to live in tents for so long. It was during this time that they, along with many other families, really had to depend on God and each other. We shared tents with three other families in the neighborhood. In such tragedies there is always strength in numbers. My brother and sister, who were twelve and fourteen at the time, were especially affected. They were forced to do a lot of growing up in a short amount of time as were all the children in the neighborhood. Instead of playing after school, they came home to do chores. My dad and his crew worked constantly to reestablish the city's power. His work caused him to be gone most of the time, but with the neighbors' help, my mother, brother, and sister were able to build a primitive wooden shack. We lived there for a long time until my dad finished building a nice apartment on the same property. From what I hear, it was a difficult experience, but it served to strengthen our family even more.

My father's determination served us well once again. He began building a larger, sturdier home, complete with a basement. It took him 11 years to finish it, but he wanted only the best for our family. My brother helped him on the weekends, and it became a great project for them. They put a lot of love and passion into finishing that home. I remember my father had to stop the work many times, because he didn't have enough money for the materials or the technical crew. But he never gave up and he saw it through to the end. One day I found him crying inside one of the rooms. He saw the

concern on my face, hugged me, and told me that everything was going to be okay. He said he was just purifying his
heart so that he could keep moving forward. I was profoundly
touched by that and I've never forgotten his incredible love
for us shown in his hard work and persistence. After several
years, my sister started working and bought the necessary supplies to help my parents finish the house. It was a time to pull
together as a family and support one another in love. My
parents needed our strength and support during this difficult
time. The responsibilities that my brother and sister received
at such a young age changed their perspective on life. They
learned to value every aspect of life and to appreciate all that
they have.

I was too small to realize what was going on. Moving into
the new house seemed great to me, but because I didn't see
the entire picture, I didn't have the same appreciation for it as
the rest of my family. Over the years, my heart has changed.
I've learned to appreciate all that I have and I understand that
everything comes from the hand of my loving God. I certainly have not "arrived." I'm still in the process of developing a
more sensitive heart. I've learned much simply by developing
a solid relationship with my parents. I have great respect and
honor for their wisdom, love, and experience. They've been
through a lot together and as they would tell you, relying on
God's love and support is the secret to their success. It's also
important for them to support each other in every situation.
In sickness and in health and for richer or for poorer, they're
together. They have their disagreements, but they never hide
them. They keep short accounts by working through things
as soon as they come up. They're not perfect, but they have
the type of relationship that I can only hope to emulate in my
marriage.

My parents have shown me how to appreciate life and how to live with love and passion. They've always said that knowing God was not about religion, but about having a love relationship with the Creator. They never imposed their beliefs on me, but they constantly encouraged me with their words and their actions. They didn't do everything right, but they never tried to hide their mistakes. Rather they let me learn from their mistakes right along with them. It's a great privilege for me to talk about them. They have always been my friends, counselors, and supporters. They had a direct hand in molding and shaping my life, setting the foundation of who I am today. I will be forever indebted for the things I've learned from them.

I believe that every generation has its own wisdom. At times their different approaches to life may seem to clash, but that's not to say that one is better than the other. Both are valuable, just different. My dad and I certainly have a different approach to things. I'm proactive and must be in constant motion to feel productive, while he's patient and takes his time to accomplish his tasks. This is exemplified in my dad's love for gardening. He'll spend an entire morning in his garden and he enjoys doing tedious things to perfection. I respect and admire that because it requires a level of patience I can only dream of one day possessing. Though I have difficulty finding joy in gardening, I've still gleaned a profound truth from my dad's passion. That is to do things to the best of my ability, not out of obligation, but to show that I have value and passion for life. My dad also taught me how to treat women. His love, care, and respect for my mom spoke volumes to me growing up. His example taught me the importance of laying aside the "macho" mentality that's so prevalent in our society – the mentality that teaches men that they rule. He taught me that love was all about getting to know my heart and sharing it with that special someone. He said that if you truly loved a woman, you would want to support her in every way and do everything in your power to enable her to fulfill her dreams. My dad is retired now. He worked 38 years for the Guatemalan Electrical Company and now he spends his time in the garden and doing maintenance on the house. He also helps one of my cousins who has a candle factory in Guatemala City.

My mom has taught me many things as well. She works as a volunteer in the cancer unit at the National Children's Hospital. She's responsible for procuring clothes, toys, and other supplies for the children. Her work at the hospital includes speaking up for the little ones who have no voice which has taught me the greatest lesson of all. We are tools in God's hand prompted by His great love. A practical way of showing our love for God is to allow Him to work through our lives to serve others. She shows people that they are valuable and that God loves and cares for them. As she will tell you, this can only be done through genuine, selfless acts. She strives to make a better life for others. She's made me more sensitive to matters of the heart. *Mami* has always been a great blessing in my life. We have a great friendship and I feel the freedom to talk to her about anything. Whether it's my goals, desires, work, or romance, she's always there to offer great advice, nothing complicated, just practical knowledge. She's a wise woman who taught me that women are a valuable blessing. I learned to communicate with women by communicating with my mom. Her point of view about life is open-minded and practical. She's always said that the only constant in life is change, so in order to be happy in life, you must always be willing to change.

Having a strong family bond is something that's insepa-rable from Latin culture, and my family is no exception. Everything is based on the unity of our family and the love we share. The tradition in my country is that you remain in your parents' house until you're married. Children rarely leave home for college and even if they do, chances are they would move back home when they were finished. Even if you have a great job and are financially stable enough to live on your own, you still remain at home. Unlike many western societies, there is no stigma attached to adult children living with their parents. I'm 30 years old, I live with my parents and I consider it a privilege to help take care of them. I've been looking for places and furniture to start a home of my own and I'm eager for such changes in my life. However, it's not because I impatiently want out of my parents' house, it's because I'm eager to start a family of my own. In fact, it will be a sad day when I leave my parents' home because I won't be as involved in their everyday lives.

My Dear Sister's Support

My sister, Annelie, is so special to me. I've learned so much from her. She's taught me that with God's help I can face whatever fears, worries, and challenges life throws my way. The 13-year difference between us has caused her to seem more like a second mother than a sister. We quickly became great buddies. She's a good listener and I feel like I can open my heart and share anything with her, having the confidence that she'll understand and give me great advice. She's always been there for me and I've learned through her that God often uses people to help us to overcome our struggles.

Growing up, one of my favorite things to do was lip-sync-ing in Annelie's room. I would pretend that I was a big star and she was my biggest fan. In my teens, I would meet her at her office on Saturdays for lunch and a movie. I looked forward to our outings because we always had a blast together. Those simple yet priceless moments we shared made me realize that women have their own strength, beauty, and magic.

At age 18, I went through a major depression. Perhaps it was the initial shock of going from high school to the real world. I was comfortable and protected at a school where everyone knew me, but that safety net was pulled out from under me when I entered the university. Annelie helped me to overcome that depression and she taught me that with God's wisdom, I could have pride and confidence in any endeavor. God has given us everything through His son Jesus. With His help, we can accomplish anything in life just as Philippians 4:13 says, "I can do all things through Christ who gives me strength." Recent proof of that is the completion of this book.

Annelie was always there to offer good advice when I was dating someone too. She taught me that there are vast differences between the way men and women think and perceive things and she often helped me to understand the female perspective. She said that women often think and feel with their hearts first and then with their minds. She introduced me to a real and practical God who is actually interested in the everyday happenings in our lives. She's always been there when I needed her. I hope and pray that I can offer the same support in her life. I'm so thankful for my sister. I know that I'm a better person because she's a part of my life. She's been a God-given support to me through the years.

> Nunca te rindas!
> Don't ever give up sister!
> ANE, YOU ROCK!

Te quiero mucho hermanita Linda!
I love you very much, my beautiful little sister!

MY EXTENDED FAMILY

When we say "family," we mean everyone, grandparents, uncles, aunts, and cousins. We actually make no distinction between immediate and extended family. Family is family. Though time is short and schedules are tight, we always make it a point to get together. It helps that most of us don't live very far away from each other.

The farthest relatives are in the U.S. My sister lives two hours outside of Houston, I have relatives in Salt Lake City and Chicago as well. My uncle, (and name sake) Gilberto, lives in Puerto Rico along with my aunt Miriam and my cousins Gina and Gessie. Some would consider this too great a distance to travel for a simple family gathering, but in Latin families, no distance is too great to keep family apart.

When I think of my family, a few special places always come to mind. One of them is our family beach home in Monterrico. We've shared so many special moments there – birthdays, holidays, and the occasional weekend get-togethers. Memories saturate that place. The many laughs and a few tears, sunburns and near drownings, wave riding and skim boarding, fire works and cookouts, and star gazing and secrets, all are recalled with such fondness. The smell of the salty ocean air always floods my mind with sweet memories of the past and gives me great hope for the future. It was during one of those blissful moments that I was inspired to write this book.

I grew up in Monterrico. Many of the cousins that I grew up with have married and now have children that they bring to our gatherings. I love playing with their kids and I eagerly await the day when I can play with my own children there and show them all the places that meant so much to me when I was their age. Because I was added to the family so late, I became an uncle in the second grade. I get teased a lot for that and the little ones call me "Uncle Grandpa" though they are actually my second cousins.

Our family is huge. When we're all together, we're about 45 people. We always get together for a big Christmas lunch. We gather at my cousin's house and as you can imagine, it's an enormous party. We share a nice meal and have a great time together, thanking God for another year of life as a family. My mom is the matriarch of the family and is usually in charge of praying for the meal. It's always good to recognize and praise God together as a family. We try our best to keep in touch between gatherings and family is always there to meet any need that may present itself. I'm grateful to have the support of my family. It reminds me that I'm not alone in this world and I never will be.

The only grandmother I had a chance to get to know was Mama Tina, my mother's mom. Her name was Josefa Cupertina Porras Lara. She was an amazing woman, so young at heart and full of life. She had five children including my mom and she worked hard to provide a better life for each of them. She was known for her great stories and her incredible memory. She never forgot birthdays and not only did she remember the day, she would often recount the entire history of the person, story after story, piece by piece. Mama Tina never had the opportunity to learn to read and write, so she asked me if I would teach her. I was very young at the time, but I was delighted to have an opportunity to help her. Unfortunately, she lost most of her vision to glaucoma before we had a chance to learn together. She passed away when she was 101 years old. She simply fell asleep and was gone. When she died, I missed her very much, but through my mourning, I learned a valuable lesson. People are a blessing in our lives that we often times don't recognize until they're gone. We take people for granted just like we take other things in life for granted. I also learned that instead of focusing on the loss of the one we love, it's better to focus on preserving their memory. It's so easy to focus on the negative and miss out on the blessing right before our eyes. There is certainly a place for mourning, but once that period is over, energy should be spent remembering what you valued most about those you loved and lost.

I also have an 'honorary' grandfather. I met him on a Saturday morning. I had just gotten back from the gym when the doorbell rang. I opened it to find a little old man with a rusted machete. He asked me if we needed someone to cut the grass. He looked weathered and tired, yet eager and not ready to give up on life. My father always cut the grass, so we didn't need his services, but not wanting him to leave empty handed, we invited him in for coffee and bread. His name was Alfonso. He was 80 years old and he didn't have a family. We visited for quite awhile and found him to be quite clever and fun to talk with. It has been over a year since we first met and we've become great friends. He still comes over for coffee and bread on occasion. Our relationship has an unusual depth and is tremendously fulfilling. He's taught me much about being kind and loving. He's the grandfather I never had. God has truly blessed my life through him. Now when he rings the bell, *Papi* or *Mami* will say, "Grandpa's here!" and we drop everything to sit and visit with him.

THE REALITY OF WAR FOR MY FAMILY

While I was growing up, Guatemala was being shaped by a 30-year civil war. Most of the intense, violent fighting took place in the highlands and families like mine who lived in the city were not directly affected. I learned at a very young age that freedom was of great value to my life, family, and country. The war claimed many lives and much of the country suffered through those three long decades.

Growing up it seemed like everything was about the war. The news reported on the latest attacks taking place in the highlands, the death toll was constantly on the rise, and entire villages were being wiped off the map. The kids in the neighborhood and I would play war. The big house I grew up in had a huge front yard that was full of climbing trees. I used to pretend I was a soldier and would set traps and make my own weapons out of wood and PVC pipe. One year when I visited relatives in the States, I came back with a plastic M-60 machine gun. My parents weren't as excited about the gun as I was. I suppose it hurt them to see how the war had affected me.

When I was around eight years old, something happened that my parents always feared, but never imagined would hit so close to home. It was an ordinary morning and I was having breakfast when I noticed my parents cautiously looking out the window. Their nervousness filled the room and there was a quiver in their hushed voices. I curiously moved closer. They were in shock and repeated over and over *"Puede esto estar pasando?"* (Can this really be happening?) That day the authorities took our neighbors away and we never saw or heard from them again. Unfortunately, this had become the reality in Guatemala. Anyone who spoke out against the government disappeared without a trace.

Another reality of the war hit really close to home for my family. My brother and sister did not have the opportunity to attend college. There were no such freedoms during the war. We did not live under a democracy, there was no freedom of speech, and university campuses were the main target for abductions as college students often spoke out defying the government. My sister was most affected as my brother was already well established in his business. At that age it was hard for me to understand my sister's frustration and her constant battle with my dad over attending university. He was doing his best to protect her, university campuses weren't safe and he feared for her life. The students' opposition of the government created a volatile environment which lead to many riots and abductions. I still remember hearing her cry at night because she couldn't go and it simply wasn't possible for her to continue her studies any other way. She was a very good student and had high hopes of earning a degree in business administration.

As I was graduating from high school in 1992, the war was winding down and I had many opportunities and privileges that were not available to my brother and sister. I remember walking down the halls and in the gardens of my private university thinking of how much my sister had wanted to get a degree. Freedom was now valuable to me and I felt it coming to our country like contractions to an expecting mother. This was the first time I realized how incredibly blessed I was. At the same time I felt a twinge of guilt knowing that my brother and sister did not have the same opportunities. One of the reasons I finished university was because I felt that I had a commitment to my sister. I didn't want to let her down and she knew I was there in part for her. To squander the opportunity that I had been given would have been a great mistake. During my first year of college my sister and I made a bet. She told me she knew I was going to drop out of university because I didn't really care about it. I insisted that I would finish and even put five hundred dollars down to prove it. Now that I have my degree, I should be collecting that money with interest. **Just kidding Sis!**

I received so many great things and opportunities growing up. I was so blessed. I'm so thankful that God has changed my heart and that I can now look back on those things with gratefulness. I pray that I may grow to the point where I always see the blessings God places in my life and that I may appreciate each moment <u>while</u> it's happening rather than in hindsight.

CHAPTER 3

SCHOOL: THE FOUNDATION OF MY LIFE

Growing up attending a bilingual school, I was constantly surrounded by an international environment. My teachers, friends, and classmates came from a variety of diverse backgrounds, nations, and cultures. I had the perfect childhood. I was admittedly spoiled, which looking back, was not the best thing for my life. My whole world was about wearing the latest styles, traveling to the greatest places, and filling my free time with entertainment. Back then I just didn't appreciate the simple things in life. Like many privileged children around the world, I was consumed with myself and my own little world. My parents worked hard to get me into a private school and I have great memories from my time there. It was a beautiful place with huge areas to play sports, large classrooms, and best of all, teachers who helped me to become who I am today. The teachers didn't just feed us factual information; they imparted morals, values, and wisdom that went far beyond book knowledge. Over the years, they became more than teachers, they became friends. One of the most

> Like many privileged children around the world, I was consumed with myself.

valuable features my school had to offer was their mix of Guatemalan and American teachers which provided a variety of views about life and culture.

In the sixth grade, students were required to take an exam which would determine who was eligible to continue their education at this elite level. This was also a way of downsizing classes as space was limited in the upper levels. The top 60% of the class was promoted to the seventh grade while the remaining 40% would be bussed to another school. It was a tense year for everyone, knowing that we needed to study harder than ever. It was particularly stressful for me because in my little mind, my entire future–all my hopes and dreams depended on the results of that exam. It was the first time in my life that I was determined to make something happen. I worked hard – harder than I had ever worked at anything before. When I found out I passed the test, I was overjoyed! I was so happy that I lived up to my parents' expectations and I was able to continue to the next level. This was my first taste of accomplishment.

When I was twelve years old, I started traveling to the United States every year between the months of October and January. My visits helped me to become fluent in English, but they also became rather routine. I didn't realize what a privilege it was to be able to travel. The majority of people in Guatemala can't afford such luxuries. I suppose most young children don't really appreciate life or recognize all its blessings – I was no exception. I usually went to Salt Lake City, Utah to visit and ski with my cousin Dave. Dave was like a brother to me and he taught me a lot about life. He always said, "You can have anything in life if you're wise, work hard, and rely on God's help." In my teens, I started to notice all of the attention he got from women. I began taking notes on the way he acted when he was with them. He was a good influence in my life and he showed me how to respect women. Now Dave's happily married to a wonderful woman named Pam. I can only hope that my life will one day turn out the same.

After a while, Utah became a part of me. I loved the mysterious mountains and the breathtaking views. When I was skiing, I was in a different world. Nature allowed me to become a part of it and somehow through the miserable cold, it was worth it. I loved to linger at the top of the mountain on the very edge, with only a few seconds to decide on the easy trail or the tough one. Once I made that decision and started downhill, there was no turning back. I loved the exhilarating rush and the ultimate control over how I maneuvered the trail. I find that life is much like my skiing experience. Everyday we face mountains and have to make decisions. Some mountains are small and we mindlessly conquer them, while others are enormous and seem impossible to maneuver on our own. But as we linger on the edge of what seems like disaster waiting to strike, it's then that our God intervenes and helps us accomplish the impossible. It's these accomplishments in life that help us to grow, make us stronger, and enable us to conquer even larger mountains in the future.

I was an average student in school, more interested in being popular and having fun, than excelling in academics. My classmates were like brothers and sisters to me. In the Guatemalan private school system, you stay with the same class until you graduate. Our schedule kept us busy. We had twelve classes because we studied everything twice, once in Spanish and then in English. I loved to participate in sports. Track, basketball, and occasionally soccer consumed my time. We even played some American football, which, as I recall, was both fun and painful.

My friends from school were awesome: Chele, Chema, El Enano, Jorgito, New Kid, El Colocho, Sancho, El Gordo, Charlie, Checks, Geto, and last, but not least, Tio Can. We called ourselves "The Lost Boys" and always enjoyed each other's company. We spent countless Friday afternoons together eating pizza, watching movies, and talking about girls and sports. We watched our favorite movie, **Space Balls**, so many times that we practically memorized it!

Unfortunately, we got into mischief too. We became professionals at stealing sandwiches from the lunches of other classmates. We researched who had the good sandwiches and dared each other to steal them. It was always fun and entertaining to me until the day I got a surprise. I found out that one of the girls had a very tempting "supreme sandwich." After a little plotting I stole it. I was so proud of myself for attaining such a prize that I didn't want to share it with anyone. As I was savoring my victory snack, all of the sudden I felt my lips go numb! My friends laughed and told me that it was a set up. They had gotten together with the girl who brought the sandwich and mixed dental numbing cream in with the mayonnaise. It was pretty funny, but painful too, I might add. But I learned a valuable lesson that day – never eat anything containing dental numbing cream!

Growing up in such a close-knit environment, it was not common to have a girlfriend from the same class or school. It was a good rule as no one wanted to disrupt our happy "family." If you had a girlfriend, she was either in another class, or she went to a different school entirely.

PATRICIA

In the 10th grade I had a girlfriend, but it was by no means a serious relationship. Her name was Patricia. She was half

Guatemalan, half American, and extremely beautiful. She went to a different high school, which made her the perfect candidate. She had long, silky, dark hair, vivid green eyes, and a certain mystery about her.

Our relationship consisted mainly of experimenting and making out. We didn't have much to say or share because as teenagers we felt like we already knew everything about life anyway. Our immaturity prevented us from making a good couple. Ours was a love that ended as soon as summer vacation was over.

CHAPTER 4

A LIFE-CHANGING EVENT

On October 16, 1990, as I was finishing the 10th grade, my life radically changed. It was a typical day. My friend Charlie came by and picked me up to go hang out with some friends. The plan was for everyone to meet at Oscar's house. Charlie and I arrived a little early, so we sat on the bumper of his Volkswagen Bug listening to the radio, waiting for the rest of our friends to show up. After a while, Oscar turned the car on to prevent the battery from going dead. However, instead of just turning the car on, he playfully took off. At first, Charlie and I thought it was fun riding on the rear bumper, but our laughter faded when we realized Oscar was going too fast. Anxious that something bad was going to happen, we started screaming at him to stop. He kept going and on one of the curves we lost our grip and were thrown in two different directions!

The next thing I remember was waking up with a bloody face at an unfamiliar house. Strangers were asking my name, where I lived, and a battery of other questions. I was confused and unsure of what had happened, but I was painfully aware of the fact that Charlie wasn't there. They took me to my house and then to the hospital. On the way to

> It all seemed like a bad dream...

the hospital I blacked out again. I woke up the next morning with one of my eyes swollen shut and the other eye almost as bad. I knew something terrible had happened because my mother was praying at my bedside. The first words that came out of her mouth were, *"Dios tiene un proposito en tu vida, no te olvides de eso!"* (God has a purpose for your life, don't ever forget that!). That was the first time I cried.

A few days later I was finally able to see my face. It was swollen, red, and mangled, and it looked terrible. The accident happened right around Halloween and the doctor teased me, saying, "Look on the bright side, you won't need a mask this year!" I have to admit he was right and that was pretty funny. That was the beginning of almost four months of total dependence. The swelling worsened and a week later my eyes were swollen shut and I was blind. Apparently, my face was the first thing to hit the pavement, and then I slid half a block. Fortunately, my friend Charlie landed on his back and only had a mild concussion – he healed with time. The doctors were concerned that I may have damaged the nerve in my head responsible for controlling eye movements. They said they wouldn't know for sure until the swelling went down. The wait was a slow, frustrating process. We were also waiting to see if healthy new tissue would develop or if I would need skin grafts and plastic surgery.

It was a difficult time to say the least. It all seemed like a bad dream. I was frustrated and afraid because I couldn't see anything. My other senses of hearing, touch, and smell soon began to compensate as they were now the only connection I had with my environment. I learned to appreciate life and people in a profound way. I had to depend on others for everything. Someone had to help me go to the bathroom, take a shower, and feed myself. I couldn't get from one place to another without making a mess along the way. It was even a struggle to cry. I was helpless.

The swelling finally decreased, but my vision was so blurry and my eyes were so sensitive to light that I still couldn't see much. During my convalescence I had to stay inside. The doctors said that the sun would cause my scarring to be worse, so for four months, my entire life was lived either in the house or at the doctor's office. I wanted to blame someone other than myself for the whole situation. My life had been so perfect before the accident. I wondered what I had done to deserve such a struggle. I simply didn't see the whole picture.

I finally healed enough to go back to school. The discoloration around my eyes earned me a new nickname, "*Mapache!*" (Raccoon!). Then the most amazing thing happened to me. To this day doctors can't explain it other than to say that it was a miracle! My eyes returned to normal with clear 20/20 vision and the tissue on my face healed without requiring plastic surgery. As I think back on the experience, I believe that the most important thing I learned was to be patient and trust that God was in control of everything. My mother was right. God did have a plan for my life, even though I wouldn't realize the extent of His plan until later – much later.

During my last year of high school, I was chosen to be part of a team of translators who helped at a United Nations (UN) seminar in Guatemala City. It was a great honor to be able to work with international agencies and UN representatives.

When we graduated from high school, doors opened easily for us. The school's reputation gave its graduates great favor in the eyes of employers and universities.

Those were special times for me and my friends and they will always be remembered with great fondness. Today, we're still good friends. We get together every month or so just to catch up. It's strange to see how everyone has changed over the years. Many of my friends are married and have children. It's encouraging to see how we've turned into responsible adults and competent professionals. Our priorities have shifted from seeking to gratify our own selfish desires to investing our time and energy into family and other responsibilities. Our view of life has also changed. We see each day as a new challenge to grow and become better people, not just an opportunity to have fun. It's great to get together to encourage one another in these things.

CHAPTER 5

UNIVERSITY: GETTING READY FOR LIFE'S JOURNEY

After high school I was ready to move on to something a little more adventurous. I didn't necessarily have a plan for my life, but I was anxious to experience new things. I was full of life and eager to learn – it was time to "find myself." I began studying in a private Guatemalan university, majoring in business administration so I could be more productive in the family coffee business. The only drawback to going to college was that I had to part with my life-long friends and schoolmates. Some started work right away and others chose to attend different universities. It was hard for me at first. I was lonely and it was difficult to get used to the university system without the comfort of knowing others were experiencing the same struggles. I knew that I would meet new people, but it was a difficult transition coming from such a sheltered environment. My friends were my family and they were all I knew. For the entire first year, I felt like the new kid on the block. I was depressed and pretty anti-social for the first three months or so. I kept to myself and didn't talk to many people. Slowly, I became more comfortable with the people around me and began to amass a new circle of friends. I discovered what a great experience it was to get to know and relate to new people. I came from an environment where my teachers knew me by name and even considered me a friend, to a place where I was no more than a number and was by no means "missed" when absent! The support and advice I was accustomed to from my teachers were no longer available and friendships were non-existent – it was strictly professional. It was difficult to accept all the changes taking place in my life, but I eventually came to realize that they all weren't necessarily bad, just different. Despite the difficult time I had adjusting, I enjoyed the new freedom I gained at the university level. It wasn't at all like high school. I didn't get in trouble for making bad grades and I didn't have a tutor constantly checking up on me. College taught me that I had to begin taking responsibility for my own decisions. Whether I was to succeed or fail, it was now my choice.

In addition to my formal education, I was learning a lot about love, relationships, and the desires of my heart. One thing that I realize now, in hindsight, is that at that time, I wasn't really ready to have a girlfriend. I only had a girlfriend because it was "the thing to do." Everyone was dating some-one and not being in a relationship was frowned upon.

My first relationship in college was fruitless, I doubt that either one of us grew from it. Sharon and I were just going through the motions together. Neither of us wanted a serious relationship so we kept things on a superficial level. We never took the time to truly get to know one another. It bordered on a complete waste of time and energy and we were pretty ambivalent about the outcome. It was like having a beauti-ful garden that you walk through everyday. You become so familiar with it that you're no longer captivated by its beauty. We took each other for granted and no longer valued one another. This attitude destroyed our relationship, but because feelings were mutual, it seemingly did no harm.

I realize now that nothing good comes from a relationship that only serves to fill an empty space in a person's life. True, society sometimes demands that this space be filled; however, a person is not truly ready to love until they are secure in themselves. When I am most satisfied with myself, then I can be most satisfying to another. I've learned that it's better to pursue a girl because she is someone special, than because I feel I **need** her.

I now know that God created us with a need for Him and completeness as a person is only found in a personal relationship with Him. It's not fair to look to another person to complete you because it's a void that only God can fill. God is the only one who can help me set my priorities and goals in life. When I am complete in Him and my priorities and goals are in line with His will, then I can have rich and meaningful relationships.

> "Thou hast made us for thyself, and our hearts are restless till they rest in Thee."
> St. Augustine

Relationships should be all or nothing. Just going through the motions is unproductive. Efforts should be made to discover the furthest corners of your partner's soul. Time should be devoted to getting to know one another and growing as a couple. We should be able to share our hearts with one another and in turn learn more about life. It's easy to find yourself in a relationship that's stagnant. You're just sitting around waiting for the miracle that never comes. Our lives are enriched by the moments we share with one another. Sharing ourselves – our goals, fears, hopes, dreams, likes, dislikes, and our very hearts – these are the things that bring value to relationships.

BRENDA

During my third year of college, I met a girl named Brenda who was in several of my classes. We got to know each other very well and she became very special to me. She had a great smile and wonderful personality. When we finally realized that we liked each other, it was an intense, dangerous attraction. We were in a vulnerable position because we could easily be hurt. Even though I really liked Brenda, I didn't want to have a girlfriend or a formal relationship. I knew that I shouldn't make a commitment if I didn't know what I wanted or didn't have the energy to contribute to the relationship. We talked a lot about our situation. She wanted to be my girl, but under the circumstances, I couldn't reciprocate. I liked her, but I knew the timing wasn't right. Something I treasure about the whole experience was the strong friendship we built. We shared our lives with one another. There was no need to hide anything because we had a foundation of trust in which we were safe and secure. Through this trust and good communication, we developed an incredible friendship.

Eventually the tension, created by the attraction between us, became unbearable. We desperately wanted to kiss, but we were afraid it would damage our friendship. We had come to a point where we had to redefine our relationship and at this point the kiss was almost inevitable. One night, we stayed after class to chat and figure things out. I was very nervous, because I knew that anything could happen and something inside of me longed to make things happen. Finally, we kissed, and it was wonderful, especially after building such a strong attraction. After the kiss, everything was different – nice, but different. We went out to lunch the next day and talked about how we felt about the kiss and about each other. I wanted to make sure we hadn't damaged our friendship. We concluded that it would be best if we just remained close friends.

Through my friendship with Brenda, I learned that all romantic relationships must be based first and foremost on a solid friendship. I needed to be honest with Brenda and protect her heart in order to show her that I really valued her. We both knew that we had different desires. Brenda wanted to have a formal relationship and I wasn't ready. She was honest with me about the fact that she wanted to be my girlfriend, but she was willing to stay simply friends. We learned much about being true friends as we studied together and supported one another. The honesty and sincerity we shared made our friendship stronger.

I learned so much from Brenda. She had great strength and confidence and she knew what she

...that's what women want anyway.

wanted in life. She also had a sixth sense about me. She could tell whether or not I was being genuine. She kept me honest and showed me the importance of being real when I relate to women or anyone else for that matter. Trying to act like the coolest guy on earth just doesn't work. Living a lie is draining and no one can keep it up forever. When you wear masks, your relationship is based on something false. It's a fragile lie that can fall apart at any moment. Not only is it easier and more relaxing to be yourself, that's what women really want anyway.

I also learned that a woman's personality is of utmost importance when considering a relationship. It's therefore critical to get to know her personality – her heart, values, and beliefs are what define her. I'm consumed with getting to know a woman's personality, the things that make her laugh, cry, or want to scream. It's like discovering a new world full of life. There are so many great things to explore, like the events in her past that have made her who she is today, her dreams for the future, and her thoughts on God, life, and the world we share. This type of sharing is the foundation of any relationship and it's a two-way street. I have to feel that she is interested in discovering these things about me as well. If we don't value one another's personalities, the relationship will come to nothing.

Upon completing my third year of college, I needed another change. It was becoming monotonous and my program of study was not everything I had hoped. It had become increasingly difficult to juggle school and my work schedule. At the time I was helping my brother with his import business. I was making frequent trips to the U.S. and driving a truck all over Guatemala making deliveries. I was missing quite a few days of class, my grades were dropping, and my professors offered little support. I decided to transfer to another university in hope of a fresh start and a program that was a little more geared to co-op students. During this transition, I'm sad to say that Brenda faded out of my life. Wherever she is, I hope the best for her. I will always cling to the lessons I learned from her. Undoubtedly I'm a better person for having known her.

Transferring to the new university turned out to be a great decision. I needed the change and was grateful for the opportunity to start fresh. Thankfully, I didn't lose any of my credits and was able to pick up right where I left off. I soon found that my new school had a much better system and was more understanding of co-op students who had to work. They were extremely flexible and even helped me stay motivated. By this time I had chosen a double major in Business and Computer Science which would take me two more years to complete. Fortunately by this time I was used to making new friends in unfamiliar places.

At the new university, I learned that it was "normal" for guys to be players. Many times I watched guys mask their true intentions. They made girls believe that they were looking for true love and a lasting

> A woman's heart is more sensitive than a rose petal.

relationship, when all they wanted was to take advantage of them. They sought to gratify their own desires and as soon as they were satisfied, they moved on to another unsuspecting victim. I was just about as shocked as the women in these situations. A guy should never play with a woman's heart - it's more sensitive than a rose petal, it has greater worth than gold, and it's sweeter than any love song. A woman's heart is to be valued, cherished, and protected. If you're honest and sincere, chances are the girl will reciprocate and there will be a mutual desire to satisfy one another's needs. We shouldn't have to hurt people to get what we want in life. In fact, true love is characterized by sacrificial giving. True love brings with it a burning desire to make another happy without the expectation, let alone the demand, that ones own needs be met.

CHAPTER 6

PASSIONATE ABOUT COFFEE

L et me tell you a little about the family business – coffee. There's more to coffee than simply pouring it from a pot to a cup as a part of a daily ritual – **much** more. Every time I drink a cup of coffee, the fragrance, the warmth, and the taste, all bring a rush of delightful memories.

In order to obtain the best cup of coffee and in turn a memorable experience, you must select a quality coffee. Being in the coffee industry since I was a kid has taught me that you definitely must not cut corners here. If you start with bad materials, there's little hope for a good experience. A worthy coffee starts with the altitude at which it is cultivated – any coffee grown above 4,500 feet is considered first class.

> *A common misconception about coffee is that acidity equals bitterness.*

Coffee is characterized by its aroma, body, and acidity. A flavorful aroma, strong body, and high acidity are all hallmarks of a gourmet coffee, and higher altitudes serve to intensify each of these attributes. Once a high-quality coffee begins to percolate, the aroma fills the air. Have you ever noticed people breathing deeply to relish the aroma? Have you noticed the smile that travels across their face as they await their first cup? Aroma can have a fragrant, flowery, or strong presence. The stronger the aroma, the more my mouth waters in anticipation of that first sip.

The body of the coffee is determined by its strength. It can be described as weak, strong, full, or even velvety. The body combined with the acidity, makes up the flavor of the coffee. The acidity of the coffee is directly proportional to the acidity of the soil in which it was grown. Acidity is said to be crisp, delicate, marked, or pronounced. A common misconception is that acidity equals bitterness. In actuality, the greater the acidity, the more pronounced the coffee's natural flavor. Coffee is bitter when it is grown at lower altitudes. Obviously, the flavor is the ultimate experience. When you take time to savor the taste and delight yourself in the aroma, body, and acidity, you begin to truly appreciate the coffee.

I love coffee and it's a huge part of my life. A Guatemalan joke is that children here start drinking coffee even before milk. I take pride in the fact that Guatemala has some of the best coffee in the world. Papi is up at five every morning to make fresh coffee to have with breakfast. Instead of donuts, we have sweet bread called champurradas. These are large, crispy, semi-sweet cookies that are broken and dunked into coffee before consumption. They're everyone's favorite and are happily enjoyed any time of day. Traditions like these unite friends and family whether for business or pleasure. Fito, my boss and good friend, often stressed and modeled the importance of enjoying the fellowship brought by sharing coffee and *champurradas. Thank you Fito for allowing me to glean this and much more from you!*

Traditions have made the Mayan people and coffee inseparable for nearly two hundred years. They do not use any modern technology. Their traditional methods have been perfected and passed down from generation to generation.

They're experts at what they do and their love and pride for family and the land are intertwined. They have managed to preserve the traditions, language, and beliefs of their ancient civilization. For instance, in some regions they still wear the typical Mayan dress that distinguishes them from the others. Their ancient culture respects and relies closely on nature. Their devotion somehow makes them a part of the land. Long ago, they developed an astrological calendar to track the cycles of the sun, moon, planets, and most importantly, the seasons. The modern coffee industry has gained knowledge from this culture that has greatly enriched their efforts and products.

> The modern coffee industry has learned much from the Mayan culture.

There are seven coffee growing regions in Guatemala based on soil type. Each region produces a distinctly different coffee. Volcanic soil produces a coffee that has a pronounced acidity and a slightly flowery aroma, while coffee that is grown in the rainforest has a delicate acidity and a fragrant aroma with a light wine note. The experienced coffee drinker can determine the region in which the coffee was grown based on its color, fragrance, and flavor.

The type of bean planted is also dependent on the soil in the area as certain species thrive in specific soil types. Each bean is precisely selected to produce healthy saplings with great potential. The saplings receive the best of care at nurseries where they await purchase. Plantation owners purchase top quality plants and each one is neatly aligned on the plantation in order to make wise use of the fertile ground. The coffee plants are protected from the sun and heavy rains by large shade trees. As a bonus, these trees produce over 5 million tons of oxygen a day all over Guatemala.

The coffee harvest is an amazing event to witness. I've come to truly appreciate the people who work on the *fincas* (coffee plantations). Whole families, including their small children pick the coffee beans. They dedicate their lives to the care of the plantation. When a bean reaches maturity, it turns red and looks much like a cranberry. Each one is hand-picked within a narrow window of time according to color and uniformity. According to the growers, these specific days are determined by the moon and other natural indicators. They say, *"Que se debe respetar la sabiduria de Dios por medio de la naturaleza,"* which means respect the wisdom of nature. The coffee beans are actually seeds that are encased in the pulp of the berry. In order to recover the bean, the berries must be de-pulped and strained using a fermentation process. This process involves soaking the berries in large water tanks until they burst. The berries that float are an unacceptable quality and are strained off. The berries that remain continue the process. Once they burst, the pulp is removed by a high pressure wash and then the beans are sun-dried. This process takes several days and requires a lot of intense work by hand. Each step is carried out according to specific protocols and standards and the greatest care is taken to produce the best product.

To ensure the coffee is fresh, every two weeks the dried coffee beans are sent from my family's plantation in the highlands to a factory in Guatemala City. At this point, they are in the "green bean stage" and must still undergo roasting and packaging. Coffee is roasted according to the desired flavor, ranging from a mild roast to an espresso. After the roasting, the coffee must be cooled. It's then packaged in special bags designed to preserve the aroma and flavor, even after opening.

My family has been in the coffee business for three generations. Many of my cousins are directly involved in growing the coffee at the family plantation. They pour great love into cultivating the best coffee possible. I am involved specifically in the marketing aspect of the coffee business. I strive, along with many others, to achieve worldwide recognition for Guatemalan coffees. Keeping your head above water in the international market is a difficult task. Marketing is a constantly changing, innovative entity in which I have found much satisfaction. The traditional method of exporting coffee is in the green stage, in bulk quantities. We export this way to various U.S. companies and others around the world; however, it's more advantageous to do the roasting and create your own name brand. This gives the coffee extra value in that it is 100% pure Guatemalan as opposed to a Guatemalan coffee bean that's been given an American or Italian flavor through a foreign roasting process.

The 3 p.m. coffee break in Guatemala is as ingrained in Guatemalan culture as tea time in the United Kingdom. Towns literally shut down for half an hour to enjoy the country's life blood. Coffee is so much a part of our lives, even American franchises have adapted to our culture. Situated between the playground and the dining room in most of the McDonald's in Guatemala is *McCafé*, a quaint coffee shop. Sitting in the café, you would never guess that you were in a fast-food restaurant as the atmosphere is worlds apart from the typical fast-food joint. McDonald's understood the cultural value of coffee in Guatemala and very strategically added this aspect to their restaurants.

Coffee is a way of life for 70% of Guatemala's population. From day workers on the *fincas* to businessmen who export coffee around the world, the livelihood of nearly eight million people depends on some aspect of the coffee industry. The state of the coffee industry became a growing concern in 1998 when international prices dropped considerably. This happened in October shortly after hurricane Mitch devastated many of our coffee plantations. The Guatemalan economy began to suffer, showing its utter dependence on coffee exports. Regardless of its status, coffee will continue to be the sole reason for countless numbers of Guatemalan people to keep fighting in life.

> Hurricane Mitch wreaked havoc on our coffee plantations.

The importance of coffee extends far beyond Guatemala reaching all over Latin America. El Salvador, Honduras, Nicaragua, and Costa Rica are substantial coffee growers in Central America, and in South America, Brazil and Colombia are the main producers. Colombia even produced a soap opera called, *"Café con Aroma de Mujer,"* "Coffee with the Essence of a Woman." It was a typical love story about a couple struggling in their life and relationship. Many of my friends identified with the story. This was amusing, considering Latin **men** do not usually watch soap operas. Evidently we forgot and just enjoyed the show! We talked about it during the week, debating what would happen next. A cousin of mine even named one of our coffee brands after the show. In the end, the couple persevered out of their love for one another. The coffee plantation contributed to their strength and bound them together. I believe that to be true in my life as well. Through good times and bad, the family coffee business draws us together and serves as a catalyst for communication and growth.

Coffee is not just another product to cultivate, it's part of our souls, it's the livelihood of our families, and it's deeply ingrained in our culture. Coffee will forever be a part of our people, our culture, and our very lives. In one way or another, a cup of coffee is involved in every special moment of a Guatemalan day. It's not just about caffeine, it's about enjoying life.

COFFEE FOR CHILDREN

Given that the coffee industry, and in turn our entire economy, has suffered greatly over the past five years, many families are struggling. Currently, over 60% of the population is below the poverty level and many of these depend on

> *It is my passion to provide opportunities for the needy children.*

the coffee industry to supply their basic needs of life. It is my passion to help change this statistic. I want to do what little I can to help the people who labor day after day on the *fincas.* I want to provide opportunities for them which will empower them to provide a better future for their children. I refuse to be just another spectator in their hardship.

One way I'm hoping to help is to partner with some friends to develop a program called **"Coffee for Children."** We have created a brand of coffee that will benefit needy children in Guatemala. A portion of the proceeds will be donated to various children's programs. Nationwide, there is a great need for children to have a better education. Programs that support children's nutrition are also vital, as there are many malnourished children who are so sick they're unable to go to school.

We must have healthy, well-educated children who will grow up to govern our country with wisdom. The future of Guatemala depends on it.

CHAPTER 7

CHANGED AT SEA

In June of 1996, while out of university classes for the summer, I received a phone call from a friend telling me about a humanitarian aid ship that was docked in Guatemala. He said they were looking for translators and he thought I might be interested in visiting the ship and applying for the job. I was interested and naturally, as a businessman, my first question was, "What's the salary?" He wasn't exactly sure, so he told me he'd find out and get back to me. He called back a few days later and told me it was a volunteer organization, and not only was there **no salary**, the volunteers were expected to **pay** a crew fee in order to live and work aboard the ship! I was not at all accustomed to the concept of volunteer work, because there are very few such organizations in Latin America. My first reaction was "Thanks, but no thanks!" and I didn't even consider it an option. My mindset was that my formal education and potential for success would be wasted if I were to work for free. Evidently, God had different plans for me. I was waiting for a response on a job I'd applied for, which I was told, could take up to a month. I was working in the family coffee business, but I wanted to try new things and was eager to experience new work environments, so I decided to see what this organization was all about.

The ship was docked in a port city about five hours away. I had no idea what to expect, but I set out with a sense of adventure and excitement. During my two week visit, I discovered the great environment aboard the ship. I met wonderful people from all over the world whose mission was to help the poor and needy by sharing the love of God in practical ways. Meeting people from different parts of the world is what interested me most during my first few days onboard. The ship traveled to a different place every few months, typically doing public relations and supply procurement in the U.S. and Europe, and outreaches in third-world countries. Along the way, the ship acquired an extremely diverse crew. Soon, the desire to help the needy, which was the adhesive among such diversity, became important to me as well. I began to long for the enthusiasm they had for God and helping others.

I worked as a translator in the optical clinic and despite the fact that I wasn't getting paid, I really enjoyed my job! It was definitely a new experience as I had never interacted with poor people before. Beggars on the street would occasionally approach my car while I was stopped at a red light, but this was as close I had ever come to the poor while I was growing up. The only help I had

> *I had never interacted with poor people before.*

ever offered was to give them my loose change. In the clinic I talked with them, asked how they felt and what their problems were. It was only about a five-minute conversation with each person, but the impact it had on me was surprisingly profound. Interacting with the people was difficult at first. I didn't know what to say and I was afraid of saying something inappropriate or giving them the impression that I thought I was better than they were. Before long, I was comfortable and interacting with them like I would with old friends. My eyes were opened to the fact that though they were poor, they were still people with hopes, dreams, and fears, just like me.

I enjoyed my stay on the ship more than I ever expected or imagined. I thought it would be a great place to work, but because the job didn't come with a salary, I was convinced it wasn't for me. I was also debating how I was going to explain this situation to my family. Didn't think they would approve of it. I was so close to finishing school and it was taking time away from my studies, not to mention the fact that I was not going to be paid. These things seemed like legitimate reasons why the ship just wasn't right for me. My family was more understanding than I expected. They were interested in hearing about my experience, but they also seemed a bit relieved that I had gotten the volunteer work out of my system.

Soon I was working at my new job in one of the biggest hotels in the city. I liked my new working environment. I was motivated in school and getting good grades. I was happy, my life was going well. What more could I want?

While I was working at the hotel, the ship was always on my mind. It had found a place in my heart. I discovered I was passionate about the work and about helping my people plus those in other Latin American countries. It was an incredible experience! But to a 21-year-old, what **isn't** exciting about living on a ship and visiting other countries? I thought about the ship often, but the fact that it was not a paying job chased away the desires of returning. After being haunted by constant thoughts of the ship, I began asking God for a sign that would help me to understand if I should return to the ship. Not too long after I began praying, I was at work when someone from administration called and asked me to take some tourists on a tour of the hotel. Being such a people person, this was one of my favorite duties. I promptly responded, met the group at the front desk, I introduced myself, and began the tour.

The group looked familiar, but I couldn't seem to put my finger on why. The chances of me knowing these foreigners were slim to none and it was driving me crazy. After the tour, we talked for awhile and I found out that they were visiting from the ship. I felt great chemistry between us as we visited over coffee; it was like we'd known each other for years. After debating for a month whether or not to go back to the ship, I was convinced that this was my sign. After all, the area was full of nice tourist hotels, what were the chances that crew members, docked nearly five hours away, would come to this particular hotel, while I was working?

I filled out the application, made the necessary arrangements, earned some money for the trip, and even received my family's approval. I joined the ship a few months later when it returned to Guatemala. Conveniently enough, they docked in Puerto Quetzal, a port city closer to my home.

My first taste of the Latin-Lover stereotype...

I had many expectations and was quite nervous because I had signed up to work for four months this time. The decision to join the ship marked the beginning of what was to be one of the most fulfilling experiences of my life.

Many things in my life changed and tremendous growth took place while I was there. This is where I got my first taste of the Latin-Lover stereotype. My interaction with the women on board earned me the nicknames "Senior Amor" and "Doctor Love." I began to understand that my friendly interactions were often misinterpreted as flirtatious, especially by western women. Though I found favor with most of the women, I couldn't help but feel there was more to their definition of Latin Lovers than the positive side they were applying to me. These realizations caused me to start thinking about what defines me as a man. I started toying with the idea of writing my life's story to somehow satisfy the longing to change this image of the Latin Lover. I started learning about how to be a better man, how to have more fulfilling love relationships, and how to respect and value the women in my life.

Life onboard the ship was great – it was like one big happy family. It was a melting pot of cultures, all connected by their bond in Christ and their desire to share His love by meeting the physical and spiritual needs of people around the world. Two of the people on the tour, Jarot and Betsy, became my first and dearest friends on the ship. They were like a brother and sister to me, making me feel welcome and comfortable from the very beginning. I was given a tiny cabin of my own. I was lucky not to have a roommate as there was very little space aboard the ship.

> The ship is a melting pot of cultures.

I was placed at the Optical Clinic to translate for the doctors as they treated the patients. I acted as the bridge connecting the two different cultures ensuring that they understood one another. I also helped to make sure the patients were getting the right prescription glasses. I enjoyed the job and I learned how to interact with older people since most of the patients were between 65 and 85 years old.

After about a month, I became more proficient at translating. Although I knew English, I didn't know the technical language specific to the Optical Clinic. I worked with Dr. Femi Oni from England, who was a wonderful doctor with a great sense of humor and much wisdom. We had loads of fun working together. We made a good team and became great friends. I learned so much from him. He had a big heart which allowed him to see every patient as an individual life and soul. He knew how to keep from getting lost in the masses and how to manage the impossible task of treating hundreds of people with limited resources. In spite of the language barrier, he was able to connect with every patient and he even facilitated a change to my heart, enabling me to see that every person was more than a name; showing me that every person was a gift from God. He showed me, by example, what a blessing and a privilege it was to know and serve each patient. It was a humbling experience to realize that I was making a difference and helping people to have a better life. I finally understood that life was <u>not</u> about money, but about having compassion, love, and understanding for others.

CHAPTER 8

A CHANGE OF HEART

Most of us never wake up in the morning and wonder if we will be able to eat that day. Few of us wander through the day with fear-

> *I had never noticed the suffering all around me.*

ful thoughts about being kidnapped or mugged. But this is the painful reality for many in Guatemala. Many struggle to survive, lacking food, shelter, and clothing, yet they never stop striving for a better life and they live in hope of a better tomorrow. I didn't grow up under such circumstances, I had no concept of poverty, and I was ignorant of the poverty that devastated the rest of my country. But in recent years, my eyes have been opened to the suffering around me.

I have also learned that there are two types of poverty: physical poverty and spiritual poverty (poverty of the heart). I never experienced physical poverty and I didn't recognize my spiritual poverty. In my mind, I lacked nothing. Little did I know that I was suffering with a heart that was impoverished and empty. I thank God for changing my attitude through the many experiences He brought into my life. He's opened my eyes to see the poverty in my own heart and He's given me a heart that now aches over the physical and spiritual poverty around me.

It would seem that as a society we have labeled people

solely according to physical standards. People that lack the basic needs of life, food, clothes, and clean water, are poor according to the world's standards. However, poverty goes far beyond the physical realm. Spiritual poverty is less obvious and more difficult to define. It reaches to the very heart and soul of every human being. It's a poverty that is placed there deliberately by the creator. It's a void that can only be filled through a relationship with the loving God. I've met people who have more money than they could possibly spend in a life-time, but who are spiritually poor. They surround themselves with everything their hearts desire, but somehow they are still overwhelmed by a void in their lives that they just cannot seem to fill. On the other hand, I've met others who are extremely poor according to the world's standards, but who have spiritual wealth unimaginable through a relationship with their loving Savior, Jesus Christ. It's through this relationship that they find fulfillment, joy, and an incredible heart to love and serve others.

My people have taught me what it means to appreciate the simple things in life. I can now sit down to a meal at my humble table and appreciate it as if it was a banquet at a fancy hotel. I've also learned that my health is a blessing that I sometimes take for granted. It breaks my heart to know that many people can't even afford aspirin, let alone treatment at a doctor's office. I desire a greater appreciation for what I have and I want to help improve the quality of life in my country. One way I can accomplish this is by doing little things that make life a little more bearable – things that bring smiles to tired faces.

This year as Christmas approached and I got together with friends to plan the usual festivities, I was overwhelmed with a sense of emptiness. I realized that we were so selfishly consumed with our own entertainment, that we neglected to do anything for anyone else. Instead of parties in fancy hotels with lots of food, I wanted to share God's love in a real way. So my friends and I decided to spend our holiday doing something a little different this time.

First, we visited 40 elderly residents at a nursing home in Antigua (about 40 minutes outside of Guatemala City). They seemed elated by our visit. We brought them a cake and a typical meal called *chuchitos.* These are similar to tamales, but smaller and covered with a red sauce. Some of the ladies I talked with were between the ages of 70 and 90. One sweet lady, Estela, really stands out in my mind. She talked with me about her life, her family, and her passion for singing. She delighted us with her still strong voice. The old songs she sang reminded me of my childhood. Generation after generation, these songs have been part of every Guatemalan child's life. She held my hand to ensure she had my undivided attention. My heart was so glad to be there listening to her sweet voice. I didn't want to be any other place on earth. In her simple way, she blessed me.

One of my friends brought his radio and we played "oldies." Though they aren't very popular with my generation, they certainly have great rhythm! When I hear music with rhythm, my body aches to respond. Before long I was dancing around the room enjoying the music. I caught the eye of a little lady who looked like she wanted to dance. She was out of her seat before I even finished asking her and she was a great dancer. There was such joy in her eyes as we laughed and enjoyed the moment.

I was thankful that I could be there serving those who felt forgotten. What a terrible thing it is to forget our elders. Their lives have such value and if we would simply pay attention to them, we could learn so much. Showing them that we cared and respected them and their wisdom was just as much a blessing for us as it was for them.

Later that day we headed to an orphanage for children 1 to 12 years old. It was run by nuns who were more than thankful for our visit. The Mother Superior told us how much the children had also looked forward to our arrival. We brought a couple of *piñatas*, a cake, and a *sorpresa* (surprise gift) for each child consisting of a bag of candy and a small toy. They were full of energy and in constant motion. We all had a blast singing, dancing, and playing with the children. At the end of the day, I realized that the best gift we gave them was to chase away their loneliness for a couple hours. Just being with them so they knew that they were special was worth far more than anything we could have brought.

If only I had more of this in my life. These are the things that give me true joy and satisfaction. It's in doing things that honor people that I have learned that love and passion go hand in hand. In order to be a passionate person, I must look for opportunities to love and serve others. I know now, more than ever, that love and passion must always be coupled with a tender, humble heart.

Everyday I pass people on the streets begging for money. I see children rummaging through the dumps in search of some small scrap to fill their aching bellies. I see tired men and women weathered beyond their years by their hard labor in the fields. I drive past the makeshift *cabanas* (shacks) that provide meager shelters for entire families. It's images like these that fuel my passion to fight for a better life

> *I see children rummaging through the dumps...*

for my country and the people I love. I want to do what I can to improve their quality of life and I've learned it starts with one senior citizen or one child at a time.

Disclaimer

Before I continue, I'd like to put a disclaimer on the following chapters. My intention in recounting the experiences I've had with love is to illustrate how each relationship has made me a better man. I do not share because I think I'm an expert in these things. In fact, I must confess that I'm still in the process of becoming the husband I need to be for my future wife. Each woman who has captured a piece of my heart and the relationship we shared, served to mold and shape me into that man. Through them I've come to have a kinder heart, to be more appreciative of the simple things in life, and to have a deeper understanding of women.

Out of the utmost respect for the women in my life, I've protected their identity by changing their names, but the feelings I had for them and the memories that I still so fondly recall, will forever remain unchanged.

CHAPTER 9

MARIANNE

The story I'm about to share is so fresh and vivid, it's almost as if it happened yesterday. It was a Friday night and I was in the dining room of the ship hanging out with my best friend Jarot. We were just killing time. I was tired and was about to go to bed when Jarot said, *"Hey Papi, ahi viene un angel en el corredor!"* (Hey Papi, there is an angel coming down the hall!) I turned around and there she was. It felt like slow motion. This girl was amazing. She had blue eyes, beautiful dark hair, and a tall, slender body. She walked by leaving me elated to have had the opportunity just to see her. Jarot and I were speechless. There simply wasn't anything to say, nothing could have added to that perfect moment.

After I recovered, I was attempting to go to bed again when a friend stopped me in the hall and invited me to a going-away party. There was a going-away party just about every Friday night on board the ship since doctors, nurses, and other crew were constantly coming and going. I decided to go to the party, which was held at one of the local restaurants. As I walked in the front door, I could hardly believe it. She was there, like a candle lighting up the room. I believe in destiny – that there are no coincidences in life and that everything happens for a reason. I would have missed so much, had I succeeded in going to bed that night, but as destiny would have it, I didn't. I was nervous, but determined to talk with her, so I found a seat nearby. I learned that her name was Marianne and that she was an optometrist from Switzerland. She was outgoing and showed an interest in my country. Of course I was happy to share all she cared to know about my life in Guatemala. We had a wonderful evening getting to know a bit about one another.

I went waterskiing all day on Saturday so I didn't see her. Water sports had become my weekend passion on the ship. I find them to be both entertaining and a huge release for me. They're one way I relax and enjoy God's creation. I've always been intrigued by the way water displays both God's immeasurable strength and His gentle peace.

Marianne and I had lunch together on Sunday. I was excited to see her again and I thought we got off to a great start. I didn't really have any expectations. I didn't want to force a relationship with her or base it on the initial, superficial impression we had formed of one another. I figured things would happen at the right moment and I wanted to be her friend more than anything else.

On Monday I was in the optical clinic preparing for the week ahead. Little did I know, it was going to be better than I could ever have imagined. I was happily surprised to find that Marianne was not only going to be a part of our team, but she was going to work with Dr. Femi and I would be translating for both of them! Working together allowed us to build a strong friendship. Although Marianne and I spent a lot of time together during the week,

> I was amazed how people from the other side of the world were teaching me how to serve my own people

we pursued our own interests on the weekends. Establishing a genuine relationship involves spending time getting to know one another. It seems that the more time you spend with someone, the greater the attraction grows.

I began thinking about Marianne a lot and I realized that I was developing stronger and stronger feelings for her. I have to admit, at first the attraction was based solely on her outward beauty, but the more I worked with her, the more I got to know her heart, and the more I got to know her heart, the more I was attracted to her inward beauty. I loved watching Marianne work with patients. She was kind and dedicated time to each person. She even practiced her Spanish on them, showing them that she was not only interested in their language and culture, but their individual lives as well. She gave them her love which in turn gave them hope. Marianne, Dr. Femi, and I made a great team. We enjoyed our work and the fellowship we shared. I was amazed at how two people from the other side of the world were teaching me how to serve my own people.

I soon realized that my feelings had gotten to the point where I needed to share them. I thought that it would be better to be honest with her, but I hesitated. I wasn't completely convinced that it was the right thing to do. One day as we were working, I just looked at her. It was one of those looks that spoke volumes. She surprised me as she looked back with a gaze of similar intensity. I looked away, suddenly feeling shy. I couldn't stand to keep looking back, her eyes were too powerful. She realized that I was struggling and repeatedly asked me what was going on. Finally, after work, I gave her an answer. I was nervous because I liked her so much, but somehow I managed to express my feelings to her. I told her that I loved how she treated people, how her smile seemed to make their sadness go away. I told her how I thought she was beautiful and how I was falling in love with her. My heart began to speak and before I knew it I had asked her if we could pursue a relationship. The moment was crushed as she told me that her feelings for me didn't extend beyond friendship. She said that she was only on the ship for a short time and didn't think it was a good idea for us to be anything more than friends. I was in shock. It was an answer I never expected and it felt as though the cabin was closing in on me. Though I was torn up inside, I respected her decision and tried to play it cool. We had dinner together, but it was awkward, it felt all wrong, and I ached to be anywhere else. I was falling for her, but she wasn't falling for me. I needed time to understand what happened and to accept her rejection.

TIME TO RECOVER

The next few weeks were difficult. I had become extremely uncomfortable around Marianne and we were constantly together at the clinic. I wanted to respect her decision. Her friendship was important to me and I didn't want to lose that, but I needed space. Being around her was too much for me, so I transferred to another clinic. Things were fine for about a week, but then they needed me back at the Optical Clinic. Shortly after returning to the Optical Clinic I had to go back to the city to take some tests at the university. It took longer than I anticipated and I was gone for

> "The ultimate measure of a man is not where he stands in moments of comfort and convenience, but where he stands at times of challenge and controversy."
> Martin Luther King Jr.

more than a week. It was a good time for me though as I needed to process all my thoughts and feelings.

When I returned to the ship, dinner was the first thing on my agenda. I caught a glimpse of her across the dining room with some of her friends. I didn't ignore her, but I also didn't pursue her. I was trying to enjoy my meal when she came over and asked if she could join me. Nervously, I said, "Sure." We talked about our weeks and she told me that she thought I left because I was running away from her and didn't want to see her anymore. I told her about the school obligations I had to attend to and, in regard to my feelings for her, I just needed some time to cool off and adjust to just seeing her only as a friend. I find this to be a difficult task. Once I start liking someone, nothing is normal. I care for them more, I see them differently, and the adventure of loving them begins. Some unseen force keeps it in perpetual motion and it's difficult to stop, let alone turn around and go back. My heart was set in motion by Marianne and things had already begun to snowball. I knew I couldn't change my feelings and go back at this point and that was my struggle.

After I finished dinner she asked if we could go for a walk on the dock and of course, I was agreeable. It was a beautiful moonlit night, a cool breeze blowing, and the sound of crashing waves echoed in the distance. She was walking slightly in front of me when all of the sudden, without a word, she turned around and kissed me! It was one of the best moments of my life. It was so unexpected, I couldn't believe it was happening! It was one of those kisses that you wish would last forever. We sat on the rocks beside the dock for a long time not saying much, just hugging, kissing, and smiling at each other. That night we returned to the ship as a couple, though we didn't talk much about what that meant for us.

The next few weeks were a blur as they often are when you're in love. We were an official couple on board and we were having a blast getting to know one another better. One day Marianne was really sick and had to stay on the ship instead of going to the clinic. I got off of work at five and went straight to her cabin to check on her. I opened the door quietly trying not to wake her and I found her lying on her bed crying. She was crying so hard that it worried me. Finally she calmed down enough to tell me what was wrong. She was sad because she realized that she would be leaving the ship soon and would miss me. She said she could hardly bear not seeing me for one day and was afraid that the distance that would soon separate us would surely end our relationship. I had been trying not to think about her departure, but as she expressed her thoughts and fears, the reality hit me pretty hard as well. She was going back to Switzerland in five weeks and my heart now demanded to be near her. That night after dinner, we found a place on the upper deck to talk about our future. We were really just searching for a bit of peace in the midst of our sadness. We asked God for wisdom and direction, knowing that we could count on Him to help us make the right decisions. We decided that it was important to enjoy our time together and not to worry about parting until it was absolutely necessary.

After that, we were able to enjoy our relationship and still talk from time to time about parting. We discussed the possibility of me transferring to a different ship based out of Europe so that I could be closer to her. We spent a lot of time talking and were able to help each other sort out many feelings, fears, expectations, and goals. The ability to work things out together is a very important aspect of a relationship and Marianne and I did it well. A love relationship involves supporting each other in life. Your significant other provides the extra strength you need to make it through your struggles. In order to make these struggles known, time must be spent pouring your hearts out to one another. Honesty and trust create the kind of atmosphere necessary for one to have the confidence to share their heart. My relationship with Marianne possessed this and more. I experienced much personal growth through our relationship and I'd like to think that she did as well.

Christmas was coming and we were planning to spend time with my family. They had visited the ship a few times and had met Marianne and some of my other friends. I showed them where I was working and explained what my job entailed. This helped them to understand the wonderful changes that were taking place in my life. Marianne really wanted to visit Tikal, a beautiful ancient town situated in the heart of the rainforest, littered with Mayan ruins, and permeated by a mysterious, majestic culture. I had never been there, but I had always wanted to visit. I was overwhelmed and happily surprised to find that she had gotten me a plane ticket to Tikal for Christmas! We went with a group of people from the ship and had a great time. Unfortunately, I was sick for most of the trip. It was awesome

> I felt like Indiana Jones...

to be able to see the jungle, animals, and ruins, but I struggled to have a good time. Finally, I started feeling better on the last day of our trip. Marianne and I were walking along a trail in the middle of the jungle when it started raining. I told her to follow me, I lost the trail, and we found ourselves in the middle of nowhere. I felt like Indiana Jones in one of his great adventures and there was something extremely romantic and exciting about it. We kissed and for the first time I felt like we were starting to say goodbye. Her departure was approaching and from that moment on everything was a little more special. We appreciated each new day a little more than the last. The simple things suddenly had greater depth and meaning. It was so hard to face the fact that she was leaving. We spent the last week in Guatemala City with my family. They were very understanding and supportive as they knew it was a rough time for both of us.

The day we went to the airport to say goodbye was absolutely heartwrenching. Both of us tried to be strong to support the other. As we ate lunch together, I was dying to stop the clock. I desperately tried to enjoy each passing moment, soaking in every last detail. The first call for her flight echoed over the PA system like a death sentence. The second rang out and we started walking to the gate. I felt like I was walking on death row. She was leaving me. We looked at each other as if contemplating a masterpiece and getting lost in its beauty, trying to engrain every little detail of one another into our memory one last time. Then we kissed like we never had before, pouring all our love and emotion into it. The final call ended our perfect moment, her hand slipped from mine, and as she began to walk away, we were unable to hold back the tears any longer. At the door, she turned around and walked backwards until she got lost in the plane. Each tear broke my heart a little more as I wondered if I would ever see her again.

I traveled with the ship for a few more months before going back to my old life in Guatemala. I needed to finish my studies and I was ready once again to begin a new phase in my life. It was hard to let go of Marianne, especially when so many places and things reminded me of her and our special relationship.

Time went by and the distance between Switzerland and Guatemala only seemed to increase with each passing day. I was never able to transfer to the ship in Europe and as we feared, the distance brought an end to our relationship. Though it was perhaps one of the hardest lessons I've ever had to learn, it was good to realize that I could survive losing someone I loved. I never tried to stop loving Marianne. Somehow I just don't think I have the ability.

Looking back it seems that the greatest thing I took away from my relationship with Marianne was the realization that every person I love is a gift from God. I've learned that we need to value and care for them and the relationship we share. Every minute that we shared helped me to realize who I really was, how I love others, and ultimately how to be a better person. I want to have the same affect on the people I love.

Marianne is still special to me after years of separation. We talk from time to time and it's wonderful to still be able to call her my friend. She's a wonderful blessing in my life.

CHAPTER 10

MISSIONS

Working as a translator for medical teams has had a huge impact on my life. These experiences have caused me to live life with a greater passion and a kinder love. They have given me a greater understanding of what it means to be a servant and a vessel through which God's love is displayed. They have shown me that this is one of my greatest purposes in life. I want to share a few of the priceless moments that have served to profoundly change my heart and life.

In April of 1997, I was working with a medical team from the States that traveled to a community seven hours outside of Guatemala City. The week-long mission was to share the love of Christ by running a free clinic at a local hospital. While I was working at the clinic translating for one of the doctors, an old lady came in with her granddaughter. She told me that they walked for three days to get there. My heart sank when I noticed they were barefoot and looked tired and hungry. The woman was 80 years old and arthritic, but still carried loads of firewood in order to make a little money for food. The doctor examined her and gave her some medicine, while I began asking the little girl what she needed. She told me that her tummy hurt a lot and after a short examination the doctor easily diagnosed her with worms. The doctor prescribed de-worming medication and vitamins for the little girl and told me to reassure her grandmother that it was normal for the worms to come out of the child's ears and nose. It was really tough to for me to translate such instructions and my heart ached for them both.

When their visit was finished, I directed them out of the hospital. My heart melted as the grandmother opened her purse and handed me two eggs. She apologized that she was unable to give us anything more. Tears filled my eyes as I thought about how valuable those eggs were to her family and how she must have cradled them to protect them from breakage over their long journey. I know that it was explained to her that our services were free, but still she insisted on showing gratitude through her sacrificial giving. I took the eggs back and told the doctor what had happened. She started crying as well and we had to take a break in order to compose ourselves, dry our tears, and get ready for the next patient.

> *Those who endeavor to invest their lives in others inevitably walk away with more than they give.*

We woke up that morning expecting to be a blessing in the lives of our patients, but we found that God's plan was to bless us through them instead. Those who endeavor to invest their lives in others inevitably walk away with more than they give.

A few years later in the spring of 2003, I joined a Catholic Medical Mission Team. I saw their ad in the newspaper requesting volunteers over the Easter holiday. I would usually spend that time at the beach with family and friends, but that year there was a strong sense that God had a different kind of celebration planned for me. I was a bit apprehensive about applying, because I wasn't familiar with the group and I also wasn't Catholic. Finally, I contacted them and they not only welcomed me, they quickly integrated me into their team. We served in a community on the southern coast of Guatemala.

I really enjoyed working with this team as I had an opportunity to talk one-on-one with the patients. I was given a little area of my own in the clinic to set up a distribution point for 250 bottles of natural tears that were donated. They were very much appreciated in this dry and dusty climate. Aside from the weather conditions, the women cooked over wood-burning stoves which also caused them to suffer with itchy, irritated eyes. The people would wait in line for the tears and instructions on how to use them. I knew that the eye drops would only provide temporary relief, but I hoped that my care and attention would make them feel special and loved. In order to accomplish this I dedicated time to each patient. At one point there were about 40 people in line, most of them mothers with their children. I tried to gain their confidence by being friendly and sincere. I had a great time with them and it seemed that each person shared a piece of their heart with me. They talked about their families, problems, hopes, dreams, and pain. In addition to giving them the tears, I demonstrated how they could find some relief in cleaning their eyes when the tears were gone. I cleaned their eye lashes with cotton soaked in clean water and instructed them that they should do it every night. It was a simple thing, but they were thankful for my time and instruction. Privately, I was the grateful one, thankful to be allowed to serve them and come away with such a great blessing.

> *Every person who has touched my heart has helped me to develop a more complete definition of love.*

Every person who has

75

touched my heart has helped me to develop a more complete definition of love. They have proven to me that life and people teach valuable lessons that could never be taught in a classroom. I have learned a great deal from watching people who are determined to succeed despite their difficult situations. Despite the right they have to complain, they still have such grateful hearts. It's my prayer that God will continue to give me a sensitive heart to learn from such people and situations.

CHAPTER 11

MUSIC AND DANCING

As a general rule, music and dancing are deeply ingrained in every Latin culture. A common misconception however, is that all Latin music and dances are the same. The truth is that distinct differences exist between each country. For instance, the way I dance Salsa is very different from the way someone in El Salvador would dance. In fact, Salsa was largely influenced by African slaves who were brought to the Caribbean (Puerto Rico, Cuba, and the Dominican Republic). The African flavor provides the interesting mix of rhythms that gives salsa, as well as other Latin music and dance, greater richness and depth.

Every country has its own musical identity which is just as much a part of their culture and history as names and dates. There's a week-long celebration of the Samba each year in its native country, Brazil. Argentina is known for their classic Tango and Mexico for their Mariachi bands. Mariachis consist of a group of 10 or more guys wearing fancy, tight costumes and over-sized hats. Guatemala has the Marimba, an acoustic instrument made of hormigo wood that is played on special occasions. My parents' generation would argue that it is an important aspect of every Guatemalan celebration.

Latin dance is becoming popular in other parts of the world as well. An annual Salsa festival is held in Japan and locals spend thousands of dollars on dance lessons, clothes, and music, in preparation for the event. Thus, Latin music is strongly influenced by culture and will continue to evolve as a result of such influences.

Music and dance provide another form of expression. Generations of Latin singers have expressed their feelings, in rhythm and song. In the 1900s, Carlos Gardel made *Boleros* popular. These are romantic, sentimental songs that are saturated with emotion. His songs can still be heard on the radio because so many people, including my parents, cherish them and the fond memories they bring.

I have so many great memories of dancing. My father started teaching me to dance when I was seven years old. He still has a lot of rhythm and good moves, even in his 70s. When he was my age or a bit younger, he danced mambo and swing. My mother says that he was incredible and caught the eye of everyone on the dance floor, especially hers. For whatever reason, God used dancing to bring my parents together – I guess He does work in mysterious ways.

As I grew up, music, rhythms, and the need to dance became an integral part of my life. Family gatherings and times shared with friends were incomplete without good dance music. In high school some friends and I

> *Family gatherings and times shared with friends were incomplete without good dance music.*

liked to learn the "New Kids on the Block" moves. We spent hours memorizing their choreographies so that we could impress the girls at parties. I've always had a great time through music and dance. Every happy moment of my life somehow involves music. My brother and sister are a bit different. They don't like to dance. Perhaps it's because we're from a different generation and they just don't feel the same about music and dancing. But just between you and me, I think it's because they don't have rhythm! *(Just teasing, as always!.)* I believe music is needed to enjoy a good time with the ones you love, regardless of whether or not you can dance.

When my grandmother turned 90, we hired a mariachi band for her birthday party. It was a huge surprise as no one told her and the band just showed up at the house. It was priceless to see her face as they walked in with their instruments in their tight flashy outfits. She danced so happily, I couldn't believe that she still had the energy and stamina for it. I think each one of us (uncles and cousins) got to dance with her that day. Since then, it's become a tradition in our family to hire a mariachi band for every birthday.

Another birthday tradition throughout Guatemala is to set firecrackers off in the celebrant's room at 5 a.m. It happens quite often and everyone in the neighborhood knows that someone's having a birthday, whether they want to or not at that hour! Luckily it doesn't happen every year, only on significant birthdays, like 30, 40 and so on.

> *Ballroom dancing is just too slow for Latin hips.*

I can dance to <u>almost</u> anything as long as I can identify with the music. I've tried with little success to identify with ball room dancing. I had this rare opportunity while I was on the ship. There wasn't much to do in the evenings, especially when we were on outreach. So when we were bored, Jarot and I would often wander the halls of the ship. One night we wandered up to the International Lounge, a medium-sized auditorium where all the formal gatherings took place. At any given meeting, there are usually no less than ten countries represented, which gives the room its name. Flags from nations around the world line the front wall and the small stage is dotted with musical instruments for the praise and worship that's a part of nearly every meeting. This particular night the chairs that usually surround the stage in a semicircular fashion had been removed and there were four couples engaged in a lesson on ballroom dancing. To be honest with you, I haven't met any Latinos who like this style of dance – it's just too slow for our hips.

Latin dances in general don't really have specific moves. Instead, you feel the rhythm and then just improvise. I like to dance salsa and mix in some *flamenco* steps. Though *flamenco* is an elegant Spaniard-style of dance and very different from salsa, it's my style and I have fun with it. I feel restricted when I have to follow certain steps or rules. They don't allow me to express myself freely. So needless to say, after ten minutes of watching the ballroom dancing, we knew it wasn't for us. They invited us to join them, but we said, "Thanks, but no thanks!"

The following week, Jarot and I asked our friend who taught the ballroom dancing if we could play some salsa and teach for a bit. Thinking no harm could be done, she happily agreed. Soon the class tripled in size and we had to move more chairs. This went on for a few weeks and before we knew it, everyone had dropped out of ballroom dancing and Jarot and I were the new salsa instructors! We were teaching about twenty couples and everyone was having a blast. I felt bad for my friend; we never intended to take over her class. We just wanted to share our culture and passion for music and dancing. It seemed to really relax people and open them up to express themselves in a different way.

Salsa is by far my favorite style

> Salsa is elegant and sensual.

of dance, although I'm really beginning to like the Tango. The major difference between Salsa and Tango is hand placement and signaling. In Salsa, my right hand is on the woman's hip and there is no sign for her to know what's coming next. It's spontaneous and sudden moves are often made when the rhythm changes. In Tango, my right hand is always on the upper part of her back and I let her know the next move by applying gentle pressure there.

My first encounter with the Tango was in 2004 when a friend of mine invited me to learn. It's the most elegant dance I've ever seen. Every move is perfect and precise. Every pass or touch of the hand tells what the next move will be in a firm, unyielding way. People who have seen it would certainly agree that it's both elegant and sensual. I understood the powerful connection that two people must have for this dance. Every move has to be perfect on both sides. The man must lead with strength, precision, and confidence and the woman must follow without hesitation. The woman always waits for the man to lead her. In order to pull it off, the two must be connected in both mind and body. They must anticipate each move. They must know what the other is thinking and be attentive to every subtle hint. I hope to share such intimacy with my future wife. Rita, thank you for the invitation to Tango!

The movie "Scent of a Woman" with Chris O'Donnell and Al Pacino gives a perfect depiction of the Tango. Al Pacino plays a blind man who, despite his handicap, confidently dances the Tango with a beautiful woman. The scene is untouchable and it's one of the best demonstrations of what the Tango is all about. The way he moves and the emotion that he invokes in his partner is amazing. Much more is going on than the dance itself. He's able to express his character and at the same time capture her essence. His disability didn't stop him from sharing his heart and soul and the dance empowered him to do so.

Another great movie that describes the passion for dancing with your heart is "Dance with Me" with Vanessa Williams and Chayanne, one of the greatest Latin performers. In this movie Rafael, played by Chayanne, moves from Cuba to the U.S. in search of his father. He never met his father and his father is unaware that he has a son. Rafael gets to the States and learns that his father owns a dance academy. He joins the academy without revealing his identity. He wins the hearts of the people around him with his humility and love. Rafael quickly realizes that the academy teaches many structured dances, but they all lack the passion and emotion that spills from the true performer's heart and soul. He becomes friends with Ruby, played by Vanessa, one of the teachers at the academy. Ruby is envious of Rafael's natural ability which seems to flow so easily from his passion for dancing. As the story progresses, they open up to one another and they begin to understand each other a little better. Rafael teaches her how to dance with passion. She learns to enjoy every move as an expression of something that's deep within her, not just for the perfection of the dance itself. I won't ruin the end for you because it's definitely a must-see movie.

> Dance as if no one is watching!

I believe that dancing is not as much about having rhythm, as it is about having fun. So my advice: dance as if no one is watching, allow your heart and soul to express itself, and above all, have fun!

Music keeps me in touch with my Latin culture and it's always been a huge part of my life. I need music to fuel my day.

It makes me happy and has the power to instantly change my mood. Whether I'm exercising, driving, or getting ready for bed, there's a rhythm in the background, opening my senses and evoking an emotional response. Music is like medicine for my heart and soul that enables me to express deep emotions, especially love. Over the years, songs have helped me to better understand love, deception, passion, and many other feelings of the heart.

Whether the music is romantic, danceable, or motivating, as long as it follows God's principles, I enjoy it. Music can have a profound effect on your heart and mind. For instance, if the music you're listening to is presenting a message that devalues women and makes them nothing more than sex objects, your heart eventually becomes desensitized to that message. Once your heart is desensitized, your mind is effected. And once both your heart and mind are affected, the message in the music is adopted and subtly played out in your life. This is a relatively new realization for me. In fact, I recently went through my CD collection and threw out all the music that did not have a message that was in agreement with God's word. Now, I only listen to music that has a positive message that will affect my heart, mind, and life in such a way that is glorifying to God.

SPECIAL SONGS THAT TOUCHED MY LIFE

Through the various seasons of my life, I've identified with different songs. When I was in high school, I dated a girl from Alabama named Amanda. She dedicated a beautiful song to me called, "**With No Explanation**" by Peter Cetera. It described what happened to us during our relationship. We became really good friends and then with no explanation and much to our surprise we began having feelings for one another. She gave me a note with the lyrics of the song. After all this time I still have that note and I can remember this song. This was the first time there was a special song for a specific time in my life.

One of my favorite songs is "**Sleeping with You**." Although the title has sexual connotations, it's actually talking about how special it is, simply to fall asleep next to the one you love. Just having that special person right next to you, heart to heart, sharing the same space, the same breath – that's what it's really all about. If you have the chance to listen to it, you won't regret it. Though it's in Spanish, you'll feel it. This is one of the songs I definitely want to share with my wife when that day comes.

I dream of one day going to a Shania Twain concert. She's so beautiful and her music and lyrics are flawless. She lets her heart control her voice and just has a way of making love sound so simple. This is illustrated in my favorite song, "**From This Moment**." I hope this special song is played at my wedding, as it would be perfect for that special moment, when according to God's word, my wife and I become one flesh. Shania you are such a *bella mujer (beautiful woman)!* If you ever need someone to dance with, I'm here!

There are so many other great songs, like "**Inside Out**" by Bryan Adams. The first time I heard it, I realized that that's were I want to be when I find the woman of my dreams. I want to get to know her in a deeper way. There are so many simple, yet powerful things wrapped up in a life. There's a unique gift to discover in each person. I know that it's only discovered by dedicating time each day to share our hearts with one another. To have a complete relationship, fit for marriage, you must get to know each other inside out.

At this moment in my life, there is a song that really describes all that I'm going through. It's a Christian song called "**Timeless**" by the group Selah. I identify with it because I'm going through a lot of changes right now. Sometimes I feel like I'm changing so much and so fast that I can't process it all. My perspective on God has profoundly changed. He's more real to me than ever before and I know He's in control of everything. I'm learning that I have to trust God in everything I do because only He is timeless. Things in my life can change as fast as the weather, for good or bad, but God is unchanging. I have to learn that no matter what the circumstance, I can rest in Him. "**Timeless**" talks about the fact that I can open my heart to life, knowing that God's hand will shield my soul.

Our hearts, souls, and lives are valuable to God. He's given us countless talents, and He wants us to use them according with His will. Music is no exception. I love to sing, but in Guatemala there is not a lot of support to develop any artistic gift so I never attempted to pursue singing professionally. I'll just have to stick with singing at church and my friends' weddings. Regardless of the level of performance, I know it's a gift that God has given me and I need to use it to glorify Him.

Whether performing, listening, or dancing to music, it will always be a part of my life. It's very much a part of who I am and it's a great way to express myself as well as my culture.

CHAPTER 12

BACK TO THE SHIP

In 1998, I obtained my degree from the university. I was elated to finally finish my formal education, though I knew that my love for learning new things would serve to make me a life-long student. I liked the City, but having completed my studies, I felt a new freedom to explore and the satisfying work I had done on the ship always beckoned me back. My heart longed to return to the place I considered my second home. My experience on the ship taught me so much. It changed my heart and my life in a profound way, giving me a whole new perspective on life. I desperately wanted more of the natural high it offered.

This time I signed on for more than a year. I joined just as the ship was sailing to Nicaragua for a three-month outreach. I was able to work in the Operating Room (OR) as a translator. Working in the Operating Room was a learning experience in itself. It was an opportunity to interact with many of the patients who came to the ship for cataract surgery. Most of the patients were grandmas and grandpas and they reminded me of my own *abuela* (grandma). Some were sociable, while others were shy, but most were willing to trust me and allow me to support them. My job included transferring the patients from the pre-op clinic on the dock to the OR on the ship's lower deck. It was a very scary experience for the patients as the majority of them had never had surgery or even interacted with a doctor. The doctor wasn't able to communicate with them directly which made the experience even more terrifying. I was the link between the patient and the doctor. I explained the procedure and how long the surgery would last. I calmed the patients down and tried to make them feel welcomed. I also answered any questions they had for me or the doctor. The patients were awake for the cataract removal and synthetic lens placement. The eye was held opened with metal clips and the doctor did the intricate work through a microscope. It's easy to see how anyone would be terrified by the whole process. During the surgery, my major focus was on the patient and how they were feeling. I gave them updates on where we were in the procedure and how much longer it would be. It was also a great opportunity to share God's love with them.

I got in trouble a few times for cutting up in the OR and earned the nickname "Patch Adams." I was explaining the procedure to a happy, outgoing *abuela* one day. I told her what to expect in surgery and then for some reason I asked her to dance with me. We only did a few moves, but all of the excitement raised her blood pressure to a level that was unacceptable for surgery. They had to give her medication to lower it and thankfully she was still able to have the procedure. After the event, I was scolded and the doctor told me that I was only allowed to dance with the postoperative patients!

The OR was a small room, full of cumbersome equipment and two narrow metal tables. In order to save time, while the surgeon was wrapping up with one patient, the nurses would prepare (prep) the next. One day, as the first surgery was coming to a close, the second patient, whom I had talked to on the dock only an hour before was brought in. She laid down on the table and the nurses began to prep her for surgery. They hooked her up to the monitors and then draped a sterile blue sheet over her. Now, only the eye that would be operated on was exposed and she was becoming increasingly nervous and claustrophobic. By this time, the first patient was being taken to recovery and the doctor began with the second. He used a local anesthetic which made her impaired vision worse and further increased her anxiety. A key part of my job was to keep the patient calm and as still as possible so the doctor could perform the delicate procedure. The patient was becoming restless so the doctor asked me to try to calm her down while the surgical team took a five minute break. I sat and talked with her and she expressed how frustrated she was with herself. She knew that if she didn't calm down, the surgery wasn't going to be possible. I felt an overwhelming burden to share my experience with blindness that followed the accident I had when I was sixteen. I told her how I was blind for several months and had to deal with similar fears. I could identify with her anxiety and I understood what she was facing. I shared how I overcame my fears by realizing that God was in control of my life and He would take care of me.

Tears coursed down my cheeks at the realization that nothing happens in our lives without purpose. Until that day, I had never understood why God allowed me to go through such a trying time. But at that moment, I realized that my period of blindness gave me the ability to identify with the people God had sent us to help. The patient was able to calm down and remain still throughout the rest of the procedure. It was a great feeling to know that the suffering I endured so many years before served to help someone else overcome a fear and rest in God's plan. I value the opportunity I had to work in the OR and all it taught me about medicine, the human spirit, and helping others.

> *"Do not forget to entertain strangers, for by doing so some have entertained angels without even knowing it."*
> Hebrews 13:2

After the outreach, we sailed to the U.S. for a Public Relations (PR) tour. No operations take place during PR tours and the need for Spanish translation isn't that great either, so I transferred to the Deck Department. As a "deckie" I did shift work, keeping watch and doing maintenance jobs. The PR tours were also a great time to see other parts of the U.S. The ship toured along the west coast procuring the necessary supplies, volunteers, and support. Once these were obtained, we sailed to El Salvador for another outreach.

During the sails, the deck department became the seamen crew so I got to learn how to watch the radar, launch the life boats, deploy the anchors, and even steer the ship! Unfortunately, I also had my first bitter taste of seasickness. I lost a lot of weight and was absolutely miserable during sails until I got the hang of it. I quickly learned that about 60% of seasickness is psychological. I discovered that if I was patient and concentrated on the task at hand instead of the unrelenting rock of the ship, I could totally suppress the nausea. Of course, the Dramamine pills that we fondly called "happy trips" also helped a great deal!

There was always something new to learn about family, fellowship, relationships, and life, on board the ship. There was a depth there that I haven't experienced anywhere else. I developed a healthy fear and respect for the ocean and its strength. Contacts were made and lifelong friendships began. I even learned how to do everyday things like laundry and cooking. As I look back, it's rather comical and a bit embarrassing that I didn't even know how to wash clothes when I first joined the ship. Growing up we always had a maid who took care of things like that, so I didn't have a clue. However, I am proud to say that after a few nearly disastrous laundry incidents, I'm quite the expert now.

TIME TO MEET KRISTA

I was cleaning my cabin one day and was startled when I noticed two attractive women were standing in my doorway watching me. I introduced myself and we started talking. Krista was a nutritionist working on her master's degree and had recently come aboard to work in the housekeeping department. Anne, Krista's best friend, would work in the carpentry shop. Both were from Norway and would be serving on the ship for a few months. I was even more startled to hear that they had heard about me in Norway! I had never been there and I knew only a few people who had. I soon discovered that we had a mutual friend on the ship. I suppose if you stay with the ship long enough, encounters like that aren't at all out of the ordinary.

We quickly became good friends. The three of us were like the Three Stooges – always together and having a blast. I could tell right away that Krista was very special. I was impressed by her heart for people. It was easy to talk to her and we spent hours doing so. I was able to share with her how much God had changed my life while I was on board. I was careful with our friendship, knowing that it could be damaged if we were to allow it to go in the wrong direction.

During that time I developed great friendships with many people and Krista, Anne, and I were part of a close-knit circle of friends. By now Jarot (my buddy from Puerto Rico)

> The three of us were like the Three Stooges!

and I were inseparable. We always had so much fun joking together. Most of the time people couldn't understand anything that Jarot said. He spoke "Spanglish," a mix of Spanish and English, very fast. I thought that was one of his most amusing qualities and I often translated for him – both from Jarot to English and Jarot to Spanish. He had a heart of gold and was willing to do anything for anyone at anytime. He was always there for us and even made himself available at all hours of the night. Though Jarot was like a brother to me, I always turned to Krista to share the things on my heart. She was a compassionate friend and a great listener. I couldn't help but feel much more for Krista than a friend should.

One night we went for a long walk and I told her how I was feeling and asked her if we could be *novios*. She told me that she really liked me, but didn't think we should become *novios* because our time together was so short. After her short stint on the ship, she and Anne were planning on traveling around Central America before heading back to Norway. She didn't think a relationship separated by such a great distance would last. I didn't know what to say. I had shared my heart and I pictured the whole thing going so much better in my mind. She was right and I felt like I had just made a huge mistake in our friendship. Sometimes I forget to think with my heart <u>and</u> my mind. I have a tendency to let my heart lead and think practically later. Though age has helped me there, it still isn't easy for me. Luckily, we were able to continue our friendship just as it was before without even a hint of awkwardness. She was a precious friend and I can't express how important it was to me that our friendship didn't suffer for my mistake.

Time passed quickly and Krista and Anne were preparing to leave the ship and begin their tour of Central America. My time on board the ship was coming to a close as well. I would be home just in time for Easter and I decided to invite Krista and Anne to visit me and my family in Guatemala for our traditional Easter celebration. They agreed and I was elated that I wasn't going to have to say goodbye just yet.

The day I left the ship, I wanted to leave behind something special for Krista so I made her a card and went into town to buy a rose. After an hour of fruitless searching, my last hope was a dollar store where I found a cheap, plastic rose. I left the fake rose on her bed along with the card and a little "it's the thought that counts" note attached.

Once home, I launched into preparing for Krista and Anne's arrival which was only a week away. I told my family all about them and their visit and was able to make plans for the day they arrived. I picked them up at the bus station and was so excited to show them the City and introduce them to *Mami* and *Papi*. The next day was Easter so we went to Monterrico to celebrate. My entire family was there and it was completely packed, so we stayed in a tent on the lawn. It was quite an adventure for me, never having been in a tent before. I still laugh as I think about the difficult time we had putting it up – talk about the Three Stooges! It took us the better part of an hour to assemble it.

> I was so lonely that I couldn't feel the magic or see the beauty in Antigua.

We had a great time with my family and Krista and Anne really enjoyed the cultural experience and the new envi-

> We must live our
> lives with passion.

ronment. They were able to see how important my family was to me. We played Monopoly until we were literally falling asleep – a family tradition. We spent our time, enjoying the beach and the pool, preparing meals, and eating. I especially enjoyed playing with my little cousins on the beach. Making sandcastles and splashing in the waves with them is something I wouldn't trade for the world! Children have a freedom that most adults have long since lost. They don't complicate things, which is something that every adult needs to re-learn.

While we were there, Anne got sick so we moved her to a bed in the house where she would be more comfortable. Everyone else had a hard day of playing and I was definitely exhausted, sunburned, and drained. I headed for the tent about nine and was asleep before my head hit the pillow. A few hours later, I was awakened by a noise behind me and as I focused my eyes, I saw Krista digging in her back pack. I had been sleeping so soundly that it took me a minute to wake up and realize who she was and where we were. When I was finally oriented, I had an incredible urge to kiss her. After a brief moment of nervousness, I made an attempt. She deflected the incoming intrusion rather skillfully by giving me a nice hug. It was clear by her actions that she wasn't going to allow me to kiss her. I felt a bit jaded, but I tried to brush it off by turning over and attempting to go back to sleep. I heard her say something in Norwegian and to this day I have no idea what it was. She hugged me again and laid down beside me. I turned over once again and looked at her for awhile. Then, we kissed. It was amazing. I felt completely overwhelmed and I knew that it was something really special. She kissed me so tenderly and then she simply smiled and went to sleep.

The next morning I was the happiest man on earth because she was right next to me. Looking at her was like contemplating a masterpiece and I got lost in it. After breakfast, we checked on Anne who was feeling a bit better so we all decided to spend the day on the beach. As the day progressed, Krista seemed more and more distant and cold. I was very confused so I asked her if she was okay. She said that she was confused about our situation and that she needed time to figure things out. We had only reacted to our emotions the night before and hadn't communicated what we wanted from one another, so the confusion was understandable and shared. I gave her some space, happy just to see how well she and Anne were getting along with my family. They were comfortable enough that they didn't need me to be around. It was a wonderful thing for me to see my family open their arms to them. They spent a lot of time sharing their lives and learning about a culture worlds apart from their own.

That evening I asked Krista if we could talk about what was going on between us so we could finally have some peace. She was dying to do the same, so we took a walk. I was shocked as she explained that her last relationship was abusive. She expressed how afraid she was to enter into another relationship. I felt honored that she would confide in me and sharing her heart seemed to help her as well. Suddenly my priorities changed. More than ever, I just wanted to be the friend she needed me to be. I wanted to help her and I was hoping that she would still allow me be a support in her life.

After our Easter vacation at the beach, we went back to the City where Krista and Anne stayed at the house with *Mami* and *Papi*. My brother suggested that we show them more of Guatemala, so we took them to the beautiful rainforest region of Coban. This area is known for its coffee and is also one of the few places left in Guatemala where the Mayan people still wear the traditional clothing. During our trip, Krista's trust for me grew and she allowed me to be more of a support in her life. We talked and shared more of our lives together and I felt we really helped each other to have a better, more complete perspective on life. One thing I realized is how differently girls and guys see and feel things. I was reminded again of the importance of good communication and the danger in assuming things are the way I perceive them to be. Krista also helped me to realize that it's important for a couple to make sure that they are both in the same place, feeling the same things.

Krista and Anne stayed for a month before they continued their travels in Central America and Ecuador. I had planned to join them in Costa Rica, but my family went through a crisis and I didn't have enough money to make the trip. It was hard for me to accept the fact that I wouldn't see them again and that I didn't have the opportunity to say a proper good-bye. Krista and Anne spent six more weeks traveling through Central America and then headed to Ecuador. After they returned home to Norway, Krista and I decided to maintain our relationship by phone and e-mail. I felt as though we should pursue a relationship and for six months or so, we did. I had shared so much of myself with her. She knew all about my life, my dreams to help other people, my vision for the coffee business, and so many other things. I felt as though our relationship was growing stronger in spite of the distance between us. I thought we were growing together as a couple and I felt as though it was time to talk about taking the next step. I knew we couldn't pursue a relationship over such a great distance and something needed to change. We needed to decide if we wanted to take it to the next level, to make it more real. I told her I could see spending the rest of my life with her. I asked her how she felt and she began to cry. It was a tender moment for us — we felt so close. She told me that she had been afraid that she was the only one who wanted a deeper relationship. We discussed the distance problem and I told her that I would like to visit her in Norway. I wanted to see her in her environment, surrounded by the things that were familiar to her. Then we could see how we felt about one another. She liked the idea, so for the next two weeks I started preparing for the trip. My family was very excited and supportive, which was a huge plus for me.

"You've got mail" never sounded so sweet!

One sunny, Saturday morning, I went to the computer lab of my university to visit some friends and check my e-mail. I was desperately hoping for an e-mail from her and the "you've got mail" never sounded so sweet. I quickly scrolled down the list for her name and my heart skipped a beat when I found it! I opened it and my whole world stopped as I read that her plans had changed. She had met a German guy and she suddenly didn't think my visit was a good idea. I felt as if my life was ruined. The room closed in on me and I was devastated. I couldn't understand what I was reading and the part I did understand, I didn't want to believe. The dreams I had about our life together were destroyed with a single e-mail.

As they say, time heals all wounds. It was quite some time before I decided that I shouldn't feel like a victim. Instead, I realized that I should remember how much I had loved her and helped her and how I had remained true to my heart. One thing I learned from the experience was that true love is strong. While we were apart, I was tempted to cheat on her as well, but I didn't because I loved her and that realization gave me a lot of satisfaction. I was pleased to see that when I love someone, I respect and value that person greatly. My heart sets my priorities and keeps me faithful.

I got a Christmas card from her that year. She tried to explain what had happened to us. She said she had gotten cold feet and just used her German friend as an excuse to prevent me from coming. I didn't want to hear it, because for me it was over. No amount of apology or explanation could have earned back the trust that was lost. We've talked a few times over the years and that's been good for me. Time has healed my wounds and allowed us to retain a casual friendship. I can honestly say that I wish her all the best in life.

CHAPTER 13

LEARNING SO MUCH

According to our relentlessly demanding society and grossly materialistic world, everything is about the way we should look and the way we should act. I've learned that my heart is the mirror that reflects my soul and many times I don't like what I see. In order to create a good reflection, I must constantly ask the Lord to mold me more into His image. I need to be more sensitive to the cries of my heart. These cries reveal the things I need to change in my life, whether it's an unhealthy habit, an impure thought, or an unfounded belief.

Lately, I've been learning that God is the best teacher in life and He's been teaching me about self-worth. I must accept myself for who I am, because God loves me as I am. My self-worth comes from who I am in Christ, not from my outward appearance. Often times we're too worried about looking good to other people. It's much easier to share our true self, than to get lost in trying to portray a false image. Most guys are immediately attracted to the perfect feminine forms, but there's so much more to a woman than her external appearance. Unfortunately, women often cater to men's desires by trying to squeeze into a generic mold. Ladies, don't be consumed with trying to have a perfect body or thinking you have to be beautiful all the time for your boyfriend or anyone else for that matter. Enjoy your life, eat right and exercise, not out of obligation, but to live a happier, healthier life. Don't get me wrong, if you like to take care of your body and you don't base your life on shallow things, that's quite healthy. I've been involved in sports since I was a kid and my week wouldn't be the same if I didn't go to the gym every morning. I eat well, but never diet, and exercise keeps me alert and in good shape. I love spinning, kickboxing, and water sports like skiing and wake boarding. I exercise, not because I have to, but because it's a release, it makes me happy, and it gives me extra energy to fuel my day.

Society has placed little value on the beauty that comes from the heart. I've met beautiful women from all over the world whose hearts were so dry and empty that their beauty was simply a glance, and sadly, after spending a little time with them, it disappeared completely. Conversely, I've met women who perhaps wouldn't turn my head in a crowd, but once I got to know them, their inner beauty intoxicated me and I became consumed by it. It's in their personality, the way they laugh, the way they talk, and the way they love and interact with others. Each woman has her own mystery and magic. It radiates from her heart and penetrates every fiber of her being. Once she's conquered her own heart, her beauty never fades, regardless of her appearance, weight, clothes, or other externals – her beauty radiates from the inside.

I don't try to keep up with the latest styles. I don't pretend to be an important person because of a great managerial position or because I have the car of the year. I want people to know me as a good friend, someone who can offer help and support. I once told a friend, *"Si puedo darte esperanza en tu vida, seré Feliz"* (If I can bring hope to your life, I'll be happy). Later she sent me an e-mail to tell me how much that phrase meant to her. I don't mean to sound arrogant, I just want to share with you what I've learned about passionately serving those around me, not out of obligation, but out of a desire to make a difference in people's lives.

A simple smile can help someone who's going through a tough time. A hug for someone you love can provide them with the strength and encouragement they need to face their fears. Don't be afraid to share your heart with the people you love. Let's be real with people and with ourselves, whether that means being more expressive with our parents, husband, or wife, or just being a good listener for our kids, significant other, or friends. **Let's go for it!**

One day it dawned on me that though my father is very special to me, I was not being very expressive with him. I realized I needed to let him know how special he was and to show him that I loved and appreciated him. Must I wait for Father's day, his birthday, or any other holiday where society says it's acceptable, almost an obligation to get him something nice and let him know how much I care? No, as soon as I feel it, I need to express it. In some cases, the opportunity may never present itself again.

So often we wrestle with our emotions and don't want to face them because they're too painful or overwhelming. We lose sleep thinking about them. We need to cleanse our hearts and souls by coming to God and letting Him work in our lives. He will give us understanding and insight into our situation. He will also put people in our lives to encourage us or even chastise us, if that's in our best interest. God has taught me so much through my married friends — through their experiences, victories, and defeats. Many of the couples have developed a greater love for each other by working through difficult times together. I've had the privilege of learning from their mistakes, perseverance, and determination. God always does what's best for us, whether we realize it at the time or not. He's had a perfect plan for me all along. He's used every experience, both good and bad, to teach me the invaluable lessons that have enriched my life. Even as I suffered through the consequences of bad decisions, God was there. He strengthened me and caused everything to work out for the best. Every experience with Him is powerful and unique. He's made me who I am today and my heart continues to desire more of Him. I want to hear His voice. I want to see His face. I want to feel His touch.

> Love is an
> incredible gift.

I realize that some of the things in this book may sound unrealistic, but perhaps that's good – perhaps we need to believe that idealistic things are just within our reach. For instance, writing this book was once just a dream. The entire process has been a wonderful adventure and I've learned so very much along the way. One of the greatest lessons has been to realize that an understanding of true love is a gift that only comes from the hand of God. Love is an incredible gift that God has given us to share with others, but it seems we're afraid to love the way we were created – to love in <u>every</u> way. Loving to our fullest potential puts us in a very vulnerable position. If you've ever given your heart to someone and been hurt, it's doubtful that you will allow yourself to be put in the same position of vulnerability, but that would be a tragic mistake. Take time to rest and heal, but don't be afraid to open your heart again. You were created to love, so love without holding back. It's understandable to be a little gun-shy, but if you don't fully surrender your heart again, you'll never truly be satisfied in any love relationship.

Sometimes we loose track in life. We find that we're just

going through the motions. We've lost that passion for life that once spurred us on. We've gotten sucked into a vicious cycle of business and we've forgotten how to really enjoy life. All our time and energy is spent preparing to live and we don't truly enjoy living. We forget the importance of people and intimate relationships. We can even get to the point where we think we have all the answers and that we have no need for God. I've been there, I know exactly what it's like, and I never want to be there again.

Now my life is different, God has given me a new direction. I'm learning so many great things about Him. I'm learning that I need Jesus' love in order to be complete in life. I'm learning what it means to depend on Him, not in a "religious" way, but in an intimate way. He's teaching me about family, forgiveness, serving others, true love, and the role he wants me to fill as a man. I feel like I'm back in school. I've just turned thirty, yet I feel like this is only the beginning of my life. Like I've been sleeping through class, and I've only recently woken up and realized I actually enjoy learning. I've already missed so much, but I'm excited to see what's ahead. All I know at this point is that no matter what, God is in control of my life. **Thank you Lord.**

> "But blessed is the man who trusts in the Lord, whose confidence is in Him."
> Jeremiah 17:7

I'm learning that trusting in the Lord is a daily process of relying on His wisdom, which is the only thing that enables me to make tough decisions. His love and passion are overwhelming. In His will, my heart is always protected. My confidence is forever in Him.

CHAPTER 14

POETRY, YES POETRY!

I started writing poetry in high school when it wasn't a very cool thing to do, especially for a guy. I was pretty secretive about it, certain that my friends would eat me alive if they found out. I learned that poetry was a great way to purge my heart of the emotions that demanded to be expressed. It was an art form – the paper was my canvas and the pen, my brush. My intense emotions painted colorful pictures of love, passion, hurts, dreams, longings, and joys. Even if the poems were never read by another person, they helped me to settle my heart and somehow define the emotions that were inaccessible by any other means. I gave some to the people close to me. The others were

> Poetry is an
> art form.

my release and my escape. The pen and paper were the only witnesses to how I felt. They provided the listening ear that my heart needed during difficult times.

Not only is writing poetry a release for me, it's a medium through which I relate my thoughts, feelings, and questions about anything that inspires or provokes me. I find inspiration in my relationship with God, in His beautiful creation, in my friendships, in romance, and in the simplicities of life, as well as the ironies. I'm comforted by the fact that with poetry, I'm free to be me, without fear of being questioned or judged.

105

The following are some of my favorite poems. It's my hope that through them you can connect with my heart on a different level and have insight into the depth of my soul.

UNEXPECTED MOMENT

On a warm and tender night I met you
Sincere feelings we shared.
Time looked like an eternity to us
I didn't know how to react.
My respirations stopped
And the rhythm of my heart took me
To an unexpected moment with you.
Life seemed so unreal.
I need time to understand
The wonderful experience we shared
Pure and natural
I saw you.
Like a beautiful flower, I contemplated you.
The most beautiful experience in my life
Was when I met you and you became a part of me.

HOW'S LIFE?

How's life? Some moments are happy, some are sad, but the worst place to be is alone. Every moment that passes in the night feels like an eternity. You're painfully aware of each breath and an eternal silence threatens to consume you. The only sound is your faint heartbeat, weak and barely pumping. Like a dying machine, it squeezes out the last ounce of feeling. Your hurting soul exhales, leaving you empty and unable to shed another tear. You're numbed by the pain that is now your only companion.

You meet someone who expresses the desire to love you and to join you in your misery. Suddenly, you're faced with a simple mathematical equation, your loneliness plus hers equals a love that lasts forever and that will grow exponentially. You give yourself to her with reckless abandon, without expecting to receive anything in return. You pour out your heart, giving her everything you can possibly give. You foolishly assume your loneliness is banished forever. Without hesitation, without considering your tenderness and love, she executes the most horrific long division. You suffer more, but why? That is the question. If you gave her everything without expecting anything in return, what was your mistake? What was your sin? You placed her on a pedestal in your heart and in a matter of days, she destroyed your dreams, your hopes, and any kind of good feelings you once had. The loneliness not only returns, it's worse than ever before.

You gave the one you thought was the love of your life, your heart, emotions, and the very things that make you who you are. And you gained nothing but her indifference? In your brokenness, you wish just one tear would be shed by the one you love. You grasp for any indication that she missed and needed you and that she was sorry for all the pain she'd put you through. You finally accept the fact that this will never be a reality. You're frustrated, hurt, and confused. You're so tired of the dark emotions that your heart barely has the strength to survive. You're so tired of being left alone in your world – the only world you have left, the only one you understand, the one that seems to suit you – a world of solitude.

Your heart has nothing left to give, yet it's anxious and smothered. It screams, "why did it have to happen like this?" You had something special – now it's gone. It vanished like dust, leaving you consumed by loneliness. Your equation was flawless, yet it was all wrong. You opened your heart so that she could understand your love and she built a wall of indifference. Her frigid response made you realize that your only option was to resign yourself to the fact that your only companion was loneliness. Loneliness was the only emotion left in your broken heart.

These are my emotions while I was experiencing a love's great power. This poem was my only form of expression and therefore, the only way to be true to my heart at the time.

TODAY MY HEART SPOKE

Today I would love to call you or just have the freedom of calling you. I long for the freedom to feel, to share, and to love without consequence. I tried to find the best solution for you and me, but nothing looked promising. When I think about you, I get lost and I don't know where to go. But I know where you are. You are there, wrapped in an impenetrable shield, like no other I've ever encountered.

It's difficult to understand my heart, when my mind is so contrary and so opposed. I long to love you with the intensity that I feel, but I don't have such freedom. I lack such pleasures. I'm hindered from being completely alive. I'm prevented from allowing my heart to indulge in you. There are so many questions, thousands to be pondered, but somehow I already know the answers. I know that I should close my heart, but it is so hard. I can't. I refuse. I want to be free. I want to be me.

I always thought that I was free to express my emotions, to follow my heart, and to truly live, but now I realize that I'm a slave. I'm imprisoned by time and circumstances. I'm not free to love you and therefore, I'm not free to express my heart and truly live. My heart demands it, but my mind warns that it's not wise. I don't know the answer and when I think I have all the questions, I find that's not the case. I don't know what to do. I don't know where to go or what to think. I don't know if my hopes can ever be a reality. I have told you before that you make me happy and I love you for that. Thank you for being in my life, one way or another. You're a blessing in my life. In spite of everything, my heart still speaks today, "I love you."

I HAVE FOUND YOU!

Yes, the woman of my life, that someone that I need every day to be happy and complete. My heart beats so intensely for you, the woman of my life. The woman who conquered all my dreams, with her beauty, passion, and smile. With your mystery so desired and special. You are the one that decides the rhythm of my heart, so perfect and tender, so real. Every sigh is a desire to have you closer, to get to know your heart. You are what I need. Life is a long journey and everything can change in an instant − I cling to that. I held tightly to that chance as I searched for a solution for you and me. A solution to our story, so beautiful and special, born so unexpectedly. But is there a solution? Is there really an answer in all of this?

There are so many powerful reasons to tell my heart to give up. The circumstances demand it and even my mind agrees that it's the right thing to do. But my love for you is so strong, I can't let you go. I won't. My heart and flesh cry out for you in an almost sinful way, but I can't be selfish. I can't. I've never been selfish when it comes to love, but I've also never loved someone this much. You're my only reality. I want you so bad, yet I must let you go. Circumstances tell me that I must. It's the right thing to do.

My heart wants to know if you really belong to me. Is it possible for me to have you, to stay with you forever, to share the love of a life time, and to finally be at rest? That's what I wish. Yes my love, that's what I wish and that wish is so real. It's as real as the fact that I have found you.

POR SIEMPRE

Es un sentimiento
indescriptible , por supuesto
Soledad, esta ella conmigo?
Tristeza, es mi realidad.
Es un sentimiento mas alla de mis fuerzas.
Es lo que recibes cuando amas alguien
y ella no esta en tu vida, nunca mas.
Solo siento mi propia respiración.
es mi única compañia
y mi corazón pregunta por ella
Ternura, cada memoria es necesaria.
cada día es lo mismo
como enfrento cada uno de estos sentimientos?
siento como que no tuviera una salida, la tengo?
mi vida sigue su camino

hay esperanza de volver a encontrarla?
lo siento pero esa respuesta solo Dios la tiene.
Y solo pienso en que no la hay, es mejor, es ser mas realista
y me pregunto como paso todo esto, pido una explicación!
Ella se ha ido de mi vida, y realmente la ame
mi amor por ella empezo como una gota de agua en
primavera
y ahora tiene la fuerza del mar.
Cada ola es tan fuerte, y demanda por ella
Su olor esta siempre en mi mente
Cada sonrisa, cada prueba de amor esta continuamente en
mi corazón
y sigue pidiendo más,
pero solo espero en ese día, donde pueda respirar
tranquilamente
espero confiado en ese día soleado,
donde podre descansar solo por Dios y su amor.

DISTANCE

Tonight the moon is beautiful, but despite its perfection, I can't appreciate it. I feel different. Perhaps it's
because "distance" is a new term for me. It's come alive.
It has new meaning and depth. According to the dictionary, distance, is the length between two points, but
in my dictionary, it's the length between two hearts.
It's hard to grasp the fact that though we live in the
same country and the same City, we're separated by
such a great distance. The obstacles are overwhelm-
ingly huge and they seem insurmountable.

Everything's changed. I did my best to analyze these

changes, to understand them, and accept them. I tried to fight them, but I can't. I get so tired of not being in control of anything. I wait for something, anything, and time goes by. I watch how the wind moves the trees and how the moon dances around my shadow. I see how the birds cuddle up and fall sleep. Time goes by without asking anyone if it's okay to do so. My mind recalls every second of you and me, the perfect moments we shared. My heart keeps beating because our love is alive, yet distance has become a new term for me.

YOU ARE MY FRIEND!

I met you under the craziest of circumstances.
And that craziness made our friendship special.
It was a Godly call as I see it long after.
When I saw you, I realized you were a beautiful person,
Not only because of your external beauty,
But because of the piercing light in your life –
That strength to change people and things.
But in those days, you were only a thought.
Time went by and experiences as well.
One day, when everything was dark and lonely,
When I felt that minutes were hours,
And my heart cried out in desperation,
God reminded me of your beauty and showed me its fullness.
He sent you to help pick me up.
To make me believe that I could walk again on life's narrow road.
Understand that craziness was more than welcomed

if it meant having you in my life.
You are among the most precious gifts God has ever given
me.
You are my friend.

LIFE

A wise man once endeavored to define life.
He searched long and hard for the best definition.
He traveled around the world researching, gathering.
He visited other wise men, debating, interviewing,
pondering, and comparing notes.
He made it his life's work and still, he felt wanting for more
information.
When he was old and ready to resign to defeat,
He walked into a beautiful forest grasping at one last thread
of hope.
He was tired and he sat down by a tree to rest awhile.
In his stillness, the beauty that surrounded him came alive.
The flowers danced to an unheard rhythm.
The wind sang an enchanting melody.
The leaves delighted him with comfort and peace.
The sun embraced these awe-inspiring things in front of
him,
And he realized his journey was over.
He happened upon the perfect definition of the meaning of
life.
It was revealing itself right there in the forest,
To anyone who would take the time to see it.
Finally he understood what life was all about:

God is life!

CHAPTER 15

THE POWER OF LOVE

In March of 2001, I started traveling to El Salvador, the small country on Guatemala's southeastern border, to try to expand coffee sales. The capital city, San Salvador, is only four hours from Guatemala City by car. I already had several large coffee buyers there and it was a huge challenge for me, but I was happy that things were moving along so well. So many surprises were waiting for me there and I never expected things to turn out the way they did. There I experienced one of the most amazing, yet misguided love stories of my life. The experience taught me much about my heart and who I am. I also learned that love is more powerful than I ever imagined. I learned that it's dangerous and I can get lost in its force, especially when I think only with my heart and not with my mind. In hindsight, I can see what a mess I can make of my life when I don't allow God to be in complete control. It's so important to trust in His wisdom and strength when my values are tested. It was a painful time in my life, but it brought about huge growth and left me with much insight into the power of love and the importance of handling its strength with care.

> Love is dangerous.

During one of my trips to El Salvador I met with the sales manager of a company I was trying to take on as a new client.

We talked about pricing, distribution, marketing strategies, and other coffee options. He was positive about beginning business with me, but he wanted me to run it by the marketing manager before any decisions were made. Since the marketing manager was out of town, we had to close our meeting without a solid deal. I returned to Guatemala frustrated that the meeting hadn't gone as I had planned. That week I called their office several times to set up a meeting with the marketing manager. She was always busy or traveling and I wasn't able to talk to her, let alone make an appointment. I was beginning to wonder if it was even worth it. I finally got the appointment and was preparing to go to El Salvador when her office called. They informed me that she had to cancel and that I would have to reschedule. I was so angry that day that I told the sales manager if they really wanted to work with me they'd better make it happen. The next appointment did work out and I finally met Andrea, the marketing manager. Our relationship was already strained because I wasn't happy with the way she conducted business, but I swallowed my pride, realizing that in order to work with her company, I needed to work with her. The first meeting was tense and I doubt that either one of us was looking forward to it. We were both very serious and defensive and I was convinced there was little hope of a good outcome. Much to my surprise, we did come to an agreement. We decided that we could work on the business proposal separately and correspond via e-mail. After a few weeks, we reached an agreement and her company started to buy coffee. It wasn't a substantial amount, but they were customers nonetheless.

During that time, my only contact with Andrea was via e-mail. If something was urgent or pressing, I had my secretary call her office. One day our communication changed. My secretary left a note on my desk for me to call Andrea. I was surprised and curious, so I called her back. The conversation was very tense and serious, composed of professional, short sentences that were in no way personal. She informed me that she was coming to Guatemala with a friend for the weekend. She knew I had a lot of contacts in Antigua and wanted to know if I could recommend a hotel. As a business favor, I made reservations for them and offered to pick them up at the bus station and drive them to Antigua. The following Friday as I was waiting at the bus stop, many questions flooded my mind. I wondered why I was waiting for her when she could have taken a shuttle. I wondered who her friend was – perhaps it was her boyfriend. I was hoping that I could impress her so that her company would buy more coffee, but was that my only motive?

When the bus finally arrived, I suddenly became nervous. I was struggling to keep my guard up – perhaps I liked her already and simply didn't realize it. As she stepped off the bus, the first thing I noticed was that her friend was another woman. Because our conversation was so short, I hadn't picked up on the fact that her friend was a co-worker and they were in Antigua on vacation, not business. As I drove them to the hotel I chatted with her friend, Nancy. Andrea was rather distant toward me and I acted the same. I dropped them off at the hotel and was preparing to leave when they asked me to join them for lunch. I stayed and had a nice time. At one point we started discussing business, but they quickly decided that it was not a suitable topic of conversation for their vacation. This was the first time they had ever been to Antigua, so I told them about the beautiful sites and recommended a few good restaurants. After some persuasion, I agreed to spend the evening with them and stay the night in Antigua. We went to a party and had a great time dancing and laughing together. I was beginning to feel much better about Andrea. We enjoyed each others company and attitudes were slowly changing between us. Nancy really helped break the ice as well.

On our way back to the hotel, we were listening to a Latin radio station and "**If She Was the One?**" by Alejandro Sanz, a singer from Spain, came on. It's a beautiful song about a man who wonders if the girl in his life is "the one," but somehow he just isn't paying attention to the signs. Nancy had fallen asleep, so Andrea and I were alone and I was singing along with the music. I felt something special and strong in that song, like I was singing it to her and the message was somehow for us. Not only were our attitudes changing toward one another, but I was sure I was starting to have feelings for her.

The next morning we had breakfast together and laughed about the night before. I went back to the City and they went back to El Salvador. That visit changed everything between us. It marked the beginning of one of the most special and challenging experiences of my life – an experience where my heart and my mind were at war with one another.

Monday morning we e-mailed each other to say how much fun we had. Soon we were e-mailing like old friends. We sent humorous e-cards to each other daily, our friendship grew exponentially, and the tension that had marked our relationship from the beginning was long forgotten. As often as I could find an excuse, I called her. I found many excuses. We started getting to know each other and talking more about ourselves. I talked about my non-existent love life and how I was enjoying being single for a change. She teased me, saying the only reason I didn't have a girlfriend was

Again the sting of the Latin-Lover stereotype!

118

that I just didn't want a serious relationship. Again the sting of the Latin-Lover stereotype and this time by a *Latina!* Then, she took me by surprise when she said she was married! I blew it off and didn't really feel the need to be careful considering we were just good friends. We continued to talk and I appreciated the connection we had. It was hard to believe that we got along so well after only a week of communication. Things were progressing fast, but I assumed that our relationship would never be more than business-casual. The reality was, the more we talked, the closer we became.

I started making excuses to travel to El Salvador on other business. Andrea and I had lunch together on a regular basis and met for coffee many times to talk "business," though our issues could have been easily resolved over the phone. We developed a great confidence and I could talk with her for hours. We talked about our goals, dreams, fears, regrets, and desires in life. We connected in such a way that we understood one another even before words were spoken. We had a lot in common. We liked the same sports, food, and activities. We shared many of the same dreams including the desire to be involved in medical missions. We often coincidently wore matching clothes and people would ask if we did it on purpose. Soon she knew all about my life. Though Andrea shared most of her life with me, she never talked about her husband. I didn't pry; I figured that I would understand that part of her life in time. The more time we spent together, the more our hearts connected, and the more complicated our relationship became.

My friends would say that they could tell how much we liked each other, but I didn't want to see it and I certainly didn't want to admit it. I think somewhere in the back of my mind I knew that if I acknowledged my feelings for Andrea,

I would also have to acknowledge the fact that I could never act on those feelings. I was beginning to see that I needed to be careful with my heart because I was getting confused. I was foolish enough to think that I was in control of the situation and my emotions, but that just wasn't the case.

> We were so naïve.
> We were so blind.

About two months into our relationship I couldn't stand it anymore, I had to acknowledge the feelings I had for Andrea. She was exactly the kind of woman I wanted, but she wasn't mine to have. After much debate, I decided it was best to talk with her. I called her one rainy Friday afternoon as she was driving home from work. I told her that I needed to talk with her about something important, but then I got nervous and quickly changed the subject. Finally, I regained courage and told her how I felt about her. Feeling the intensity of the conversation, she pulled over. She told me that I needed to remember that she was married and that I was only a good friend to her. I reassured her that I wasn't expecting her to react any differently and that I just needed her to help me deal with my emotions. I told her that we needed to be careful in our relationship, because I was feeling this way. We talked for a long time and the conversation turned out to be a lot less intense than I expected. We decided that we needed to talk in person so we met at a Mexican restaurant. I felt like it was my first date and I didn't have any idea what to say or do. We were both extremely nervous, but by the time the waiter finished taking our order we were comfortable once again. Andrea admitted that she was feeling the same attraction and she agreed that we needed to be extremely careful. But the more we talked about our feelings, the more comfortable we became with the situation. Soon the tension was completely gone and we were laughing about it.

To this day, I don't know how either one of us could have been so naïve as the think that we could handle the situation as friends. We were so blind. We refused to face reality and we underestimated the power of love. I left the restaurant feeling as though I was walking into trouble, but I refused to turn away.

We continued to spend a considerable amount of time together. One day in particular vividly stands out in my mind. Andrea traveled to Guatemala and we had lunch in Antigua. We walked all over Antigua until we found ourselves at my favorite hotel. It was both sunny and cold, which created a delightful atmosphere at the monastery ruins surrounding the hotel. We were tired and found a bench where we rested a while.

A tone of seriousness came over us as we shared what was on our hearts. I told her that I felt like we needed each other, but that such a need could never be filled. She said she felt the same — she was much happier since she met me, but our intensifying emotions were making it too dangerous for us to be together. Though I was dying to kiss her, I told her that I thought it would be best if we didn't see each other anymore. I didn't want to make her question her marriage.

Seconds were dragging by and it felt as though my heart was going to pound right out of my chest. I leaned toward her, focusing in on her lips. I hesitated. For the first time in my life, I stopped myself to think

> "There are dire consequences of stifling the still small voice of God within us."
> Fran Sciacca

about whether what I was about to do was right or wrong. *"Besame,"* (kiss me) she said. I replied, *"Si te beso, sera como abrir la corriente de una presa de agua, nunca podremos controlar esa fuerza."* (If I kiss you, it will be like breaking a dam and we won't be able to control the strength of the water.) Again she said, *"Besame,"* and I did. It felt like my first kiss. It was gentle and tender – one that gives your heart away. I kissed her again and then we just held each other. We reacted to the intense emotions of the situation and afterwards we realized that we had crossed the line. We had entered a different world. We were both nervous and happy at the same time. It was an awkward delight.

That night, we went for dinner, but maintained our distance. We were in shock because we finally realized the trouble we were in. I dropped her off at her hotel and I went back to the City. The next morning she went home. After that, things were awkward between us. We kept talking and we even talked about how we felt about the kiss. We both loved it, but at the same time we were very worried about getting lost in the situation. It was clear that we loved seeing each other and spending time together. I was falling in love with a married woman and that definitely was not a good thing.

One day she finally told me about her husband and their marriage as it was something I needed to know. She told me that she and her husband dated for almost five years before they got married. They had been married for three years, but their connection was gone and their perspectives on marriage were very different. They were going in opposite directions. She felt he was more concerned about his job than he was about her. She was hurt and felt like he had forgotten her. She said that she tried to express her feelings to him, but he only communicated with her when it was absolutely necessary.

Andrea needed loyal and honest support and she wasn't getting it from her husband. I needed to be able to share my heart with someone and I was able to share with Andrea at a deeper level than any

> Nothing was clear anymore...

other person on earth. So she looked to me to fill that need to be heard, loved, and cherished, and I looked for the same from her. We didn't know how to do the right thing. Our hearts and minds were in constant conflict. Our lives were so much easier before we met. A lot of tension was building, especially for Andrea. She was always worried about being caught and I knew that she was suffering because of me. Nothing was clear anymore – nothing made sense.

We attempted to end the relationship several times without success. Once we even managed to stay away from one another for a whole month. Not a day went by that I didn't want to call or e-mail her. I woke up many nights thinking of her, my feelings were so intense. I couldn't figure out how to start my life again. Our distance was important as Andrea needed time to fall in love with her husband again. After that seemingly endless month, we got together in a small café in a hotel in San Salvador. The plan was to reassess the situation and decide if our relationship was over or if she was going to start ending her marriage. I thought for sure that I was going to lose her. She needed to make so many changes in her life in order to be with me.

In Latin America, divorce is not well accepted by family or society. I was only in favor of it because I was blinded by my love for Andrea. My biggest concern at that time was that if she asked for a divorce, her family might oppose her. It's devastating to have that kind of pressure from family and society. I was nervous as I sat across from her in the café. The final decision was up to her, but I secretly hoped in my heart that she would choose me, of course.

We started by talking about how much we had missed each other and how we realized that our forced absence had only served to strengthen our love. She said that her life had been much more peaceful during that time because she didn't have to hide things and there wasn't a constant fear of being caught. Listening to her, I gained a greater appreciation for the freedom I had to follow my heart, but at the same time I realized that it was a false freedom. The truth was we had no freedom because what we were doing was utterly wrong. Our relationship could never be right the way it was.

Finally, she broke the news that she had decided that our relationship would have to end. Though I halfway expected it, the reality was earth shattering. She said she needed to give her husband another chance in order to have peace in her heart. Though I was writhing in the pain of heartache, I respected her decision. I supported her because I loved her. Unconditional support is one of the hallmarks of true love. I left the cafe broken and dreading the consequences of loving someone who was not mine to love. I was facing great loneliness again and my heart was heavy.

> The passion drained from my life.

During the first few days, I felt as though I was living someone else's life. Things seemed so surreal. It was too difficult to deal with my emotions, so I shut down. I was numb and life seemed to go on without me. The passion and the very essence of who I am seemed to be drained from my life all at once and I was only an empty shell. During that time I identified with a song by Daniel Bedingfield called "**If You're Not The One**." It's about a man passionately pursuing a girl that, for whatever reason, he can't have in his life. The chorus was the cry of my heart for Andrea. I felt like she was the one made for me, but she was just beyond my reach.

"I don't want to run away but I can't take it, I don't understand.

If I'm not made for you then why does my heart tell me that I am?

Is there any way that I can stay in your arms?"

About a week after our breakup, I got a call from Andrea! It was 4 a.m., but she knew I would be up getting ready to go to the gym. I was surprised that she was calling me at all, let alone at that hour. She was sobbing and told me that she couldn't live without me. She said she loved me more than ever and I told her I felt the same. She said she wanted to see me so badly, so we got together later that week. We didn't say much, we just kissed and held each other and said how much we loved each other. It was a perfect meeting. For the first time in our relationship, we didn't care if people saw us. Our love had grown deeper than I thought was possible. My wounds disappeared when she was close to me and I realized how much I needed her in my life. We completed each other. We could have been the perfect couple had the circumstances been different. Instead, our relationship was ridden with guilt and frustration. Andrea and I were able to support each other in our individual lives, but the painful reality that we weren't free to have a life together, always seemed to remain just below the surface. Though life always seemed like a sunny day when we were together, the reality was quite different. Nothing about our relationship was right. It was this reality that we both refused to acknowledge. We never wanted to end our relationship. The times apart were merely our failed attempts at doing the right thing. I prayed many times for help and forgiveness. I asked God to give me wisdom to know the right thing to do and the strength to do it.

Looking back, it almost seems impossible for love and wisdom to coexist. Ending the relationship was our only option and, in actuality, it never should have started in the first place. The only way to make things right at this point was to break things off completely. But that was definitely easier said than done.

Andrea often talked about her family. She had a great relationship with her mother and sisters. It was nice to hear her stories and to know that her family was an important part of her life, but I only got to enjoy Andrea's family from a distance. For obvious reasons, I was never able to be a part of family events. I often felt like I was getting the leftovers. In many ways, I was just a spectator in Andrea's life – I was an outsider. The only exception was when she introduced me to Veronica, her best friend from college. It was nice to meet her, I had heard so much about her from Andrea and I knew she was the only one who knew about "us." I liked her even more when I learned that she was supportive of our relationship.

We planned a get-together at a hotel in El Salvador. Veronica was going to be Andrea's excuse to get out of the house. The plan was flawless, but it didn't work out. The day I was getting ready to leave, Andrea called me and said that she wasn't going to be able to meet us. Veronica had already headed to the hotel and she said that I should go and meet with her. When I arrived at the hotel, I found Veronica, but it was strange to meet her without Andrea. We talked over dinner about Andrea and her life. It really helped me to see things from a different perspective. I saw the pressure that Andrea was under in a whole new light. Veronica told me that she couldn't believe Andrea was seeing me. She said that Andrea was always the "good girl" at the university and that no one who knew her would ever have dreamed that she would have an extramarital relationship. I also met Veronica's family. They really liked Guatemala and wanted to hear all about my life there. They asked me if I had a girlfriend back home and I felt ashamed as I quickly answered "No." Veronica and I went shopping together and bought something for Andrea. She was a good friend to me that weekend and it was no surprise that she and Andrea were such close friends. Though I didn't see Andrea that trip, I somehow felt closer to her because I got to know her through Veronica. I left with a better outlook on our relationship than when I came.

I talked to Andrea the following Monday and told her how my weekend with Veronica went. I teased her saying that I was glad that I passed her friend's test and that she approved of me. Then she told me why she hadn't been able to meet us. She said that her husband blatantly asked her if she was cheating on him. She denied everything, but the incident really made her think twice about our plans. It was as if he knew something and that really worried her.

We talked all week but Friday when I called her she was very cold to me. She said she couldn't talk because she was really busy. She had never reacted like that before; she seemed like a totally different person. When I hung up I knew something was really wrong so I e-mailed her. I asked her what was going on and if she was OK. She e-mailed me back saying that she was scared because her husband told her to be careful with her cell phone bills. He hinted that a lot of information could be found out through them. That afternoon she called to say that she needed some time to figure things out, but that she would call me soon to tell me how things were going for her. Again she sounded like a different person. She was tired of living a lie, constantly having to cover things up. I could understand that, but as I hung up I felt like we were in two different places. Something in her voice just seemed so different.

A week passed and she called me to say that she wanted to talk to me as soon as possible. I told her that if things were going to end, I at least wanted to talk to her in person. Evidently she had different plans because she told me everything right then on the phone. She said that she needed to make a lot of changes in her life and I was first. She wanted to give her husband another chance and she couldn't do that with me in the picture. I just listened to what she had to say. She was so clear and determined. I told her that I loved her and I asked her if she loved me too, but I never got a response. The silence said everything and it was one of the worst experiences of my life. I guess I always knew that our relationship would eventually come to an end, but I never expected it to end like that, without feeling or compassion. I had always supported Andrea and all I ever wanted was for her to be happy, even if that meant being with her husband instead of me.

> I had played with fire and gotten badly burned.

I learned that loving her meant that I had to be unselfish, accepting the fact that her happiness may not be found in relationship with me. I think she was harsh because she wanted to make sure that I wouldn't try to keep her in my life. Her actions made it so clear. That day I felt sad and lonely, but more than anything else, I felt betrayed. In my pain I finally realized what had happened. I had played with fire and had gotten badly burned. I knew there was a risk all along, but I didn't heed the warnings.

I needed to cleanse my heart and I wanted to understand why things ended the way they did. I e-mailed Andrea and asked if she was attempting to hurt me in hopes that I would never care for her again. I felt like an old discarded toy. I didn't actually expect to get an answer from her, I just needed to let my heart speak. Cleansing my heart after a bad experience helps me to forgive and find peace without growing bitter. Bitterness contaminates others so easily and, more often than not, it only hurts the people that I love the most. Much to my surprise, she responded. She told me that I was right and that she wanted me to hate her and finally be finished with her. She thought that it would somehow make things less painful. She deliberately showed no emotion, and broke things off in the harshest way possible. She wanted to call me and explain things better and I reluctantly agreed. We talked on the phone and I told her how I didn't understand why she sounded so different that day. She wasn't the same woman I had fallen in love with. I poured my heart out and told her how she made me feel in those brief heartless moments. She apologized for hurting me. I never wanted to complicate her life or make it worse, but in many ways I did just that. It was good to talk with her and we needed that closure in order to have peace. That was our last phone call.

Our lives diverged and we headed in different directions. I heard that she found a new job and I stopped doing business in El Salvador altogether. We got together for coffee earlier this year. We caught up a little and talked about the happenings in our lives. She told me that the song, **"The Reason"** by Hoobastank, was just for me. She said that she was sorry for the pain that she had caused and she thanked me for the motivation that I brought to her life to be a better person.

*"I want you to know, I've found a reason for me to change who
I used to be.
A reason to start over new, and the reason is you.
I'm sorry that I hurt you, it's something that I must live with
everyday.
And all the pain I put you through,
I wish that I could take it all away.
And be the one that catches all your tears,
and that's why I need you to hear."*

One thing I realized in hindsight was that Andrea never entirely expressed herself to me. She held back an entire part of her life and I saw how that affected our relationship. Though I had given her all my heart, she never truly gave me all of hers. Not that her heart was mine to have, but a relationship where feelings aren't mutual can never thrive. We were able to talk about that and she agreed that it was true. She said that she was constantly struggling with feelings of guilt and she knew that in order to give her heart to me completely she needed to end her marriage. She knew that she wasn't giving herself fully to anything in her life. It had to be an all or nothing decision and she was stuck somewhere in between. I never understood that, perhaps I needed to be in her shoes to understand. Maybe this was just one way in which we differed. If I don't share the things in my heart, I'm restless, without peace, and miserable. I think that she was just tougher than me in that regard.

The time that Andrea and I

> But despite all the special things we shared, we were so wrong.

spent together was special in many ways. We got a taste of how intense, powerful, overwhelming, and unbelievable love can be. But despite all the special things we shared, we were so wrong. We were so utterly blind. I learned a lot from this painful time in my life, but I learned it the hard way. I learned that relationships can never be based solely on love. In order to have peace in a relationship, it needs to be based on doing what's right. We needed to obey God's rules for our lives regardless of the love and attraction we had for one another. God designed love and relationships, and He has established rules for those relationships in order to protect our hearts. He doesn't want us to go through unnecessary pain and suffering because our hearts are precious to Him. True love only comes from God. He blesses relationships that are conducted in His way. Andrea and I never had the freedom, stability, or peace that were necessary to grow together as a couple because we weren't following God's plan. No one could have possibly won in our situation. Everyone got hurt. I thank God for being merciful to us and for showing us the right way even after we made so many mistakes. Now that my wounds have healed and scared, I can honestly say that I hope Andrea has a blessed marriage.

CHAPTER 16

PAY ATTENTION GUYS

There is a danger in viewing intimacy and relationships as a game or just a means to have a good time. It's easy to fool around with women and have one superficial, meaningless relationship after another. It feels right for the moment, but time is fleeting, feelings change, and in the end all that remains is emptiness. I've learned that in order to value my heart and soul, I must avoid such relationships. This has been one of the best decisions I've made for my health and my future. I know that God has someone very special for me and I need to wait on His timing.

As I've mentioned before, I went against my better judgment in my relationship with Andrea. That situation damaged my heart and scarred my life in more ways than I ever imagined. I want to warn guys in similar circumstances. If you're falling in love with a married woman, there's only one solution. **RUN AWAY!** Never look back. It's not worth it. No one wins and, without a doubt, everyone involved in the situation gets hurt.

The greatest lover ever, Jesus Christ, has given us the ultimate example of what it means to love genuinely and passionately. His example is graphically depicted in Mel Gibson's movie, "**The Passion of the Christ**." It was Jesus' great love that drove Him to the cross where He willingly suffered and died for you and for me. Jesus gave us this example, not only to show His love for us, but to show us how to love one another. God commands husbands to love their wives just as Christ loved us (Ephesians 5:25). God has a special plan for each one of our lives. They're good plans that will bring us success, hope, and a future (Jeremiah 29:11-12). Our part is to simply pay attention and wait patiently for God to reveal His will for our lives. It's not always easy to follow God's will. In fact, at times God may bring tests and trials into our lives. But He never does so without a purpose and He always has our best interest in mind.

Sometimes I wonder if I'm willing to follow Him, especially if it means that I must go through tough times. That's where I am right now. I've chosen to follow Him with all my heart, no matter what and I'm facing one of the most difficult, yet rewarding, times in my life. He's teaching me to trust Him with every detail of my life. He's showing me how to be a real "lover of life." This verse describes my current reality and it has helped me to persevere through difficult times.

> *"Blessed is the man who perseveres under trial,*
> *because when he has stood the test,*
> *he will receive the crown of life*
> *that God has promised to those who love him"*
> *James 1:12*

Seeking God is a great adventure. He is the only way to eternal life. Any trials that you may face along the narrow way are well worth it. We all mess up and make mistakes, but God is willing to invest in our lives and help us overcome any obstacle. Let Him touch your life, you'll never be the same again.

Though it is totally unrelated

> *Seeking God is a great adventure.*

to Latin culture, the movie "**Braveheart**" also depicts a life lived with love and passion. I identify with the main character, William Wallace, who was a warrior who fought for the freedom of Scotland. His purpose for fighting and his principles were always so clear. It wasn't about power, land, or wealth. It was about regaining his God-given freedom. His beloved was killed and he suffered her loss, yet he never gave up. His passion made him stronger and he understood the purpose of his journey. He knew his only choice was to fight. Surrender was not an option, so he stood against his enemies, the English. He knew his cause was supported by God and he was even willing to give up his very life for what he believed. He knew that his heart and soul would live on, even after his death. Like Wallace, we need to have a brave heart to follow God's will in every aspect of our lives and to fulfill the purpose that He's laid out for us. We need to have a steely determination about life despite the hardships we face. We must rely on Him and never give up.

THE BEAUTY OF A WOMAN

I enjoy looking at a beautiful woman. I like to contemplate her hair moving in the wind, the way she walks, the way she smiles, and the way she views life. Her beauty goes far beyond her outward appearance. Each woman has her own beauty, strength, and mystery. They deserve to be appreciated and respected.

> *The physical side of love is a glorious gift from God.*

Woman was God's perfect gift to man. He chose to bring forth life through them. I was amazed when I discovered the Song of Songs in the Bible. It's a beautiful poem that depicts the physical side of love. Its sensual narrative applauds sexuality as part of God's amazing creation. God created us to be passionate lovers, but only with our spouse. He wants us to enjoy sex in celebration of marriage because that is the place it can be most enjoyable and fulfilling. This passage from Song of Songs gives a small taste of the amazing passion between lovers in God's will:

> *"Let him kiss me with the kisses of his mouth –*
> *for your love is more delightful than wine.*
> *Pleasing is the fragrance of your perfumes;*
> *your name is like perfume poured out.*
> *No wonder the maidens love you!*
> *Take me away with you – let us hurry!*
> *Let the king bring me into his chambers*
> *We rejoice and delight in you;*
> *We will praise your love more than wine."*
> *Song of Songs 1:2-4*

THANKS TO ALL THE WOMEN

I want to take this opportunity to thank each of the women that made this book possible. Once again, I'd like to thank my dear *Mami*. Without her, my life would be empty and my heart would be void of love and passion. She taught me to seek the Lord in a REAL way. I thank Marianne for her friendship and for keeping in touch all these years. I wish her the best of luck in Nicaragua. I thank Kristina for being honest with me, even when it hurt. Andrea, though we did things the hard way, I'm thankful for all that we learned. I'm most thankful that God enabled us to finally have freedom from our relationship.

Every woman who has been a part of my life is special to me. I loved each one of them in a different way. It's been a joy to share our stories and the things we learned from each other. Despite the pain that may have occurred during our relationship, there were more happy moments than anything else. The way each woman shared her life with me and the way they trusted me to take care of them was such a blessing. I'm sorry for all of my mistakes and I beg forgiveness for any hurts I may have caused.

CHAPTER 17

THINGS I KNOW TO BE TRUE

Never get married because you're in love." I laughed at my friend's absurd statement, but he stared back at me with utter seriousness. I was seeing Andrea at the time, my heart was demanding her, I loved her and I thought I needed her. What I really needed was a greater understanding of the true foundation of lasting relationships. At first that simple statement sounded inconsistent and contradictory, but then I understood the profound truth it contained.

The majority of couples, when asked why they want to get married, say rather robotically, "Because we're in love." However, this is a big mistake. You should never get married <u>only</u> because you're in love. It sounds crazy and I was rather shocked to realize it myself, but it's true. Think about it. Love alone, is not a good enough reason to get married. A relationship built only on emotions will never endure for a life time – so much more is required. My desires can deceive me; they're not the best resource to make decisions on what I need in life. God knows exactly what's best for me. I've learned that the only way I can develop a lasting relationship is to seek God's wisdom.

Love is the **result** of a great marriage and a great marriage involves hard work and commitment. A successful relationship is not only about love, it's about being prepared for a journey that will involve more than just emotions.

A relationship is like a coffee tree. If the basic needs of sun and water are not supplied to the tree, it will never produce good coffee. First it will stop growing, then the beans will fall off and the tree will be rendered totally unproductive. At this point it's only a matter of time before it dies. A relationship is the same. A few key ingredients are needed in order to have a healthy, productive relationship. Good communication is as vital to a relationship as the sun is to plants. Having a shared purpose in life and similar interests are important as well. Personalities must also be compatible and the two must share a common moral and ethical code which shapes the way they view life and death. When these basic ingredients are present, then a relationship has the environment it needs to grow, flourish, and be productive.

Communication is the essence of a relationship. Being able to freely share my heart is something that's very important to me. In order to feel comfortable and at peace in a relationship, each person must always be able to communicate openly with their partner. A

> "There is no greater lie than a truth misunderstood."
> William James

person should never be punished or hurt for expressing how they feel about the relationship. A mutual trust must be present to accommodate this open, honest interaction. The analogy that I want to create for the special person in my life is that I'm like a big, fluffy bed where she can always find rest. I want to be a place where she is able to share her heart without hindrance. This type of confidence and security is only found through good communication.

Prospective partners must have a common purpose in life. Your hopes, dreams, and goals don't have to be identical, but you must at least be headed in the same direction. Too many marriages are made up of two people growing in different directions. In order to have a functional marriage, I need to know what my partner wants out of life and we need to be on the same page. Having common interests helps. After all, fifty years is a long time to live with someone with whom you have nothing in common. How your time, energy, and resources are spent will be directly determined by your interests. If your interests are not similar, you can guarantee that there will be a constant battle. Spending time with one another, whether it's eating, shopping, traveling, playing, walking, dancing, or making love, is a vital part of growing together as a couple. Intimacy, even in everyday activities, is crucial. It's through the seemingly insignificant activities that you grow closer together toward a common goal.

> "Love does not consist in gazing at each other but in looking together in the same direction."
> Antoine De Saint-Exupery

I found that it's not wise to base a relationship solely on what I feel. I need to consider our future together and make sure that we can grow in the same direction. This can be one of the most frustrating parts of building a relationship as it takes time to realize where you are with your partner and it often involves denying what you want in order to meet your partner's needs. As a couple, we must be patient and wait on God's timing. When we wait on Him, he will reveal the direction He would like us to take. And it's that direction that will bring Him the most glory and us the most satisfaction in life, both as individuals and as a couple.

Personality is perhaps one of the first things we notice about a person, yet it's also one of the last things we truly get to know. People are multifaceted and it takes time to explore their depth and the furthest corners of their character. Our moral values and ethical code defines much of our personalities, yet are a point of contention in many relationships. They shape the way we conduct our lives, not to mention how we raise our children. Getting to know the personality and the values of the one you love is of utmost importance. This is where the most time should be spent. Through good communication and time spent doing things you both enjoy, getting to know each other will happen naturally.

There are several areas in a woman's personality that I'm drawn to – areas that I find extremely attractive. One of the most important things for me to determine is if she is growing on a personal level. Is she trying to improve herself both outwardly and inwardly? Does she periodically make assessments of her progress? Does she make slight adjustments here and there in order to become a better person? I also want to know if she's materialistic. I look at where she spends her time, money, and energy. I'm not very interested in a woman who believes that bettering themselves only involves the external – having the latest styles or making the most money. This type of person is constantly gaining more, but they're never satisfied or content with what they have. I'm looking for a woman who's grateful for what she has and who's content with her life, but not to the point of complacency. I want a woman who not only realizes that there is a deeper meaning in life's happenings, but who also searches them out. I also look at the way she treats others, whether she values and respects people regardless of their position or status in life.

I note the way she treats everyone – strangers, waiters, taxi drivers, children, the elderly, and the beggar on the street. I want to see if she shows gratitude, respect, and compassion. If she doesn't have gratitude for strangers who are serving her, why should I believe that she'll appreciate me when I serve her? It's important to treat people with the respect that they deserve. I not only want to see how she reacts to people who are serving her, I want to see how she serves others. Serving people is very important to me.

I need a woman who values people as much as I do and sets the same priorities in life. I believe that the single most important thing in a marriage is the ability to give without expecting anything in return. There's a certain vulnerability involved in giving, and unconditional giving is the evidence of true love. It's about yielding to another person, giving them your whole heart, and sharing it freely with them. I'm looking for a woman who enjoys sharing with others, gives freely of herself, and who will trust me with her heart.

> *"I am my lovers and my lover is mine."*
> **Song of Solomon 2:16a**

Undoubtedly there will be things about that special one that you won't like – little things that get on your nerves. You must decide if you're willing to live with these flaws. Marrying someone under the assumption that you will change them is not a good idea. It's very likely that both of you will change;

> "Your willingness to accept the differences between you will allow you to complement one another in ways that make life better for each of you."
> C. W. Neal

however, marriage is not a conditional commitment. Love should be unconditional. If I can't completely accept the one I love, just the way she is, I had better think twice about marrying her. If we can't accept each other's <u>entire</u> personality, idiosyncrasies and all, then we're not ready to get married.

Time always gives me the best answers. I appreciate the love, courage, and passion that women bring to life, but now I realize that I have to wait on God's timing to enjoy these things to the fullest. I ache to have a family of my own and often times the wait frustrates me. These are the times when I just have to slow down and remember that God is in control and He's not going to let me down. It's so important that I be sure that the woman I chose to marry is the right one. I need God's wisdom to do the right thing. I don't think dating has to be difficult or tricky, but it's absolutely essential that I think with both my heart <u>and</u> my head. I can't rely solely on my emotions because infatuation truly is blinding.

Falling in love is a bit scary and I continue to ask God for wisdom in that area, but I trust that the day will come when all of these ingredients come together in the perfect proportions. I will meet the woman of my dreams. We will share many of the same interests and we will be called to fulfill a common purpose in life. We'll make the perfect playmates and we won't have difficulty communicating because we'll have enough confidence and trust to share our hearts freely with one another. Our personalities will be perfect compliments, such that it will be difficult to tell where she stops and I begin. I will learn from her and she from me and somehow, in the end, we will both have a clearer picture of life and of God.

I have heard that true love only comes once. It catches us by surprise like a blow from behind and truly sends us head over heals. It puts a constant smile on our face and our whole world could fall apart without interrupting our sweet delight. It consumes our minds and we find it difficult to focus on anything else. When the whole world pales in comparison to the one who holds your heart, then you can dare to say, "I've found the love of my life." When I wake up with a wedding band on my finger, I will be confident that I made the right decision. There will be no uncertainty, because I will have based my decision on these things and not solely on my emotions. I will roll over and gaze into the eyes of the woman my heart loves and know that I have been truly blessed.

"He who finds a wife finds what is good
and receives favor from the Lord."
Proverbs 18:22

CHAPTER 18

QUESTIONS & ANSWERS

As I got more into writing this book and more in touch with my heart, I wanted to know what questions women had about Latin Lovers. So I started to ask my non-Latina friends, who in turn asked their friends and so on. For the most part, they wanted to understand more about the Latin culture as a whole. I thought it would be enlightening to include a few of their questions and my answers.

Q "Do you ever mean what you say?"

A Yes, I always mean what I say. I never say anything just to look good or to score points. If I don't feel it in my heart, it doesn't get past my lips. At the same time, if something is on my heart and in my mind, I can't hold it in, I have to express it. It's about being passionate about love and love is always honest.

Q "Would you know someone was right for you the moment you saw her or would she just be another woman to romance?"

A I don't really believe in love at first sight, but I certainly believe in an initial reaction or chemistry. If I see a beautiful woman, her external appearance may cause a rush of emotion or even a physiological response. I get nervous,

147

my heart rate and respirations increase, and I begin to sweat; however, I believe that this is more accurately defined as infatuation, not love. Often times, I meet a beautiful woman and I find that her external beauty fades when I discover her shallow character. Suddenly any infatuation I felt disappears. Right now I'm not looking to have just another romance, I'm seeking God for the woman who's going to complete me as a man. I'm hoping that my next book will be the greatest love story of all – the process of meeting my wife and becoming one.

Q **"If you decided that a girl was something wonderful and you wanted to marry her, would it change your lifestyle or would it scare you away?"**

A Neither really. If I met a girl I was crazy about, I would share with her who I really am. If she felt the same way, then she would love me for who I am, not for who I could be. I wouldn't need to change my entire lifestyle. I feel the need to change when God works in my life, revealing things that don't measure up to His standards. God may use a woman to accomplish this, but I would never change just to impress a woman – those kinds of changes never last. I also wouldn't be scared away. In fact, if I knew she was the perfect marriage partner and I had God's approval, I would pursue her and make sure she got to know my heart and my life in an honest way.

Q **"What do you think your life will look like after you are married?"**

A I would like to have a big house with a huge yard, perhaps in a small town somewhere in the mountains like Utah or Colorado. I'd like to be in a place where my wife and I know everyone. I dream of opening a quaint little country restaurant with her. There we would sell great food and, of course, the very best Guatemalan coffee. Our 2 or 3 kids would help us with the business and add such richness and depth to our lives. We would enjoy life together, grateful for the blessings God has given us. I know we would make a difference in the world by serving God and the people around us. I realize that God may have different plans for my life, and I'm open to whatever He wants.

Q "How do you define marriage?"

A Marriage is one man united to one woman in a commitment before God. A friend once told me, "marriage is like a massive ocean; although it's full of water, it still needs a tear drop every single day to prevent it from drying up." Sometimes they're tears of joy and other times they're tears of heartache. But the bottom line is that marriage is about being committed to working things out everyday. It's hard work, but that's what I'm looking forward to sharing with my future wife.

"For this reason a man will leave his father and mother and be united with his wife, and they will become one flesh."
Genesis 2:24

Q "Will you be faithful?"

A This is a really good question – one that I have asked myself. Yes, I will be faithful. Faithfulness is not only influenced by one's culture, it's also dependent on a person's core values. Faithfulness asks if you really love the person and if you'll be true to the promise that you made before God and man. As you've read, I've been in a situation where unfaithfulness was an issue. I went out with a married woman which was certainly against my better judgment. Even though we never had sex, we fell in love and we allowed a bond to form that never should have formed – one that was extremely difficult to break. It wasn't a good experience for anyone involved. We needed to stop the relationship and we needed God's forgiveness in order to be blessed by Him. It was only by His grace that we were able to walk away. Looking back, I learned that unless a marriage is built on a foundation of Godly principles, it's fragile, unstable, and vulnerable to unfaithfulness.

Q "As a Latino, what is your ambition?"

A As a Latino, I want to put my culture up high for the rest of the world to see. I want to share the things God has taught me about being real and living a better life. I want to be able to serve others in a practical way. I know I can only do these things with a God-given passion for life and sensitivity for people. By far, my greatest ambition is to have a family of my own through which I can accomplish these things.

Q "Why does it frustrate you to be called a Latin Lover?"

A Being called a "Latin Lover" doesn't frustrate me. Rather it challenges me to share my perspective (as a Latino) on Latin Lovers. I do this with my words and my actions. My aim is to correct the misconception many people have about Latin Lovers and Latin Culture in general.

Q "Can you teach me to dance like that?"

A Absolutely, I love to teach women to dance. I've noticed a lot of women, especially North Americans, are so concerned with doing the dance well, that they forget that it's all about having fun and being happy. The only way you'll become a great dancer is to use less mind and more heart. When I'm in love, dancing is another way to express how I feel about that special person. When you put your heart into it, it becomes more than a dance, it's a form of expression.

Q **"Why are you so passionate, but don't want a commitment?"**

A This is a really good question. I can't speak for other Latin guys, but I'm passionate about every aspect of life, not just romance. When you live each moment with passion, it shows that you have a greater appreciate for life. Right now, I'm learning how to be passionate about getting to know God in a deeper way. God is the only one that can change my heart; in fact, He already has in the area of commitment.

I was once scared of commitment. I can't remember how many times I thought marriage wasn't for me, especially in my university days. I wanted to be passionate, but not committed. Now that I'm 30, I can honestly tell you that I ache to have a family and someone with whom to share my life. I believe that's what the Lord wants for our lives – to be happy with our families.

Themes surrounding marriage, faithfulness, commitment, and family surfaced again and again in this question and answer session, confirming the obvious reservations women have about Latin Lovers. Many believe these essential things are of no interest to Latin Lovers, when in actuality, the opposite is true. I long to be married and start a family, but without faithfulness and commitment to my responsibilities as a man, God will never bless anything I do.

CHAPTER 19

THE GREAT BEGINNING

A s I sat down to write this final chapter, I reflected on how much my life had changed since I started the book. God, in His great love for me, stepped into my life and it changed in the exact way that I needed. I don't mean to sound overly religious by any means. Unfortunately, being "religious" has gained a negative connotation in recent years. Rather, I want to share how my life bares witness to the fact that there is a God who is alive and powerful. He's a God who regularly steps into the lives of ordinary people, overwhelms them, and leaves them changed forever. I experienced this profound transformation a few months ago and I'm not the man I used to be.

To be honest with you, when I started writing this book, my heart was in the wrong place. I had selfish motives and it was purely for my own gain. The book was my way of escaping from so many things in my life. I shut God out of the picture and I was determined to do my own will. But then I began to see that He had so many greater purposes for this book, not to mention for my life. So I placed each page in His hands, I invited Him to join in the adventure, and we completed it together. He's transformed it into what it has become and in the process He taught me so much about life and having a relationship with Him. He gave me a better perspective on the past and a new direction for the future.

I had the opportunity to finish this last chapter at Lake Atitlan, a beautiful lake two hours northeast of the City. I traveled to San Antonio Palopo, one of the twelve beautiful towns surrounding the great lake, as part of my job with the Presidential Commission for Local Development. No matter how many times I see the lake, I'm still awestruck by its beauty. Yet, this time it was like I was seeing it through someone else's eyes. There was a depth I never noticed before. I was suddenly not only basking in the beauty of the place, but I was rejoicing in the One who created it and who allowed me to be there to appreciate it.

"The heavens declare the glory of God;
the skies proclaim the work of his hands.

Day after day they pour forth speech;
night after night they display knowledge.

There is no speech or language
where their voice is not heard."
Psalm 19:1-3

As I made my way down the hallway of the school, I came to a veranda overlooking the lake. The sun caught the water at just the right angle, turning it into a silvery sheet of glass. The piercing blue sky contrasted with the fluffy clouds that seemed whiter than white. The three volcanoes that loom over the lake with a certain air of authority were still shrouded by the morning haze. The jagged, stately cliffs endured the relentless lapping of the tide and the thick foliage masked the other eleven towns surrounding Atitlan. I had to stop and capture the moment. The scene was imparting an overwhelming amount of inspiration. It was taking over and

I had to let it. I opened my lap top, hoping that I would have enough battery to capture all the thoughts and feelings that flooded my mind. Moments like this remind me that love and passion will always be a part of my life.

A child timidly approached me. He seemed puzzled and rightly so, I guess. He had probably never seen a laptop, let alone a strange man typing away on one in the courtyard of his school. My fingers couldn't keep up with the experience. It was a bit cold at that altitude, but the sun warmed the air to a tolerable temperature. The air was crisp and seemed cleaner than any other place in Guatemala. I shot a mischievous smile toward the boy and he smiled back. I asked him what his name was, but he just peered back at me blankly. A teacher, who had witnessed the entire event, explained that considering the boy's age he probably didn't understand Spanish. He only spoke *Cackchiquel,* the tribal language of the Mayans in that area. Despite the boy's inability to communicate with me, his curiosity forced him to linger, mesmerized by the computer screen. The teacher's curiosity was also raised and she provided me with a desk and a power source for my computer.

It was wonderful to be able to serve at their school as a part of my job. Unfortunately, most people can't identify with me when I say that I'm so passionate about my job that it doesn't even seem like work to me. This is definitely one of God's greatest blessings in my life. For the past year I've worked with the Presidential Committee bringing aid to needy communities. It's a privilege to be able to help people have better lives and impart hope to their often grim situations. My job was to access the potential of projects proposed by the locals which would serve to bring jobs and revenue into their villages. I was part of a team that traveled to underserved areas listening to the ideas of the people. We would make suggestions on how to improve their ideas and we acted as middle men to put them in contact with the necessary people and organizations that could help them make their dreams a reality. The Commissioner over this department, Fito, believes that our people need only to be empowered in order to have a better life. The potential is there, they just need a bit of a push, a word of encouragement, and the materials to stand on their own. As part of the project in San Antonio Palopo we wanted to help the local school. The buildings were old and tattered and really needed a face lift. We were able to help by painting a few of them. Many people combined their efforts to make this happen and I was touched by their hopes, dreams, and determination. Unfortunately, this was my last trip with the Commission, but it was a great project to end on.

The sun gradually danced around my shadow and the school became deserted. The sound of children laughing and playing was replaced by the wind and the voices of a few song birds that it carried. Being in the mountains always makes me feel closer to God. I peered down the hill at the town below. Kids were running in the streets, happy to be finished with another day of school, people were about their daily chores, and smoke from wood burning stoves rose from each house. Everything seemed to be in perfect working order.

I was coming to so many conclusions about my life. A slight breeze caressed my face and carried with it the sent of a wood fire. It reminded me that love needs to be stoked with tenderness and dedication. As long as it has fuel, it will burn with strength and determination. This and so many other profound analogies cried out to me from

> *Yes!*
> *Latin Lovers*
> *really do exist!*

that incredible vista. Among them was a conclusion to the question posed in the very beginning – Latin Lovers, do we really exist? Yes! Latin Lovers really do exist, but we are not defined or recognized by the stereotype that has been widely accepted. I asked people all over the world to define the Latin Lover. Most of the definitions I received were shallow, undoubtedly based on society's misconceptions and lies. The following definition however, stood alone, far above the rest.

THE BEST DEFINITION EVER

"My definition of a Latin Lover comes solely from my experience with and observation of the only Latino in my life. If I could stereo-type all Latin Lovers based on my scrutiny of him, it would be more than a compliment. I think the typical image the world has placed on Latin Lovers is one of heated passion, centered around the sexual experience and outward appearance, giving little account to feelings of the heart and long-term commitment. Such a shallow definition seems to devalue the romance of this passionate culture and does not begin to adequately describe what I have observed.

The Latin Lover I have had the privilege of knowing is full of passion and has depth far beyond the first impression. He longs to provide for the daily needs of the one his heart loves – to protect her, to grow old with her and to empower her to reach her dreams. He aches to become a father and is already making plans for the future arrival of those who will call him *Papi.*

Do these things make him any less sexy or passionate? If anything they should make him more so. He has life in proper perspective. Though the temptation is there, he chooses not to gratify his passions with frivolous relationships. He seeks a Godly woman who will support him when he is weak and allow him to lead when he is strong. He's willing to work for her and he enjoys the challenge of an endless pursuit. He's willing to take risks, yet he cautiously prepares for the future. His unexplored dimensions make him mysterious, but his willingness to be venerable allows him to be known. And amazingly, he has insight into the most guarded heart – my own. Undoubtedly, as he continues to seek God's will, he will be blessed with a wife that perfectly compliments him. It is my prayer that the world's definition of Latin Lovers would one day reflect what I know to be true." (Lori)

I believe this definition captures the essence of the true Latin Lover. It may make them sound a bit fictitious, but I feel it perfectly describes the Latin Lover that I long to become. I struggle each day to live up to such a definition, but I know that through God's strength, I can.

*"I can do all things through Christ
who strengthens me."
Philippians 4:13*

GOD IS SO REAL!

I always knew that God was there for me, but I was so caught up with living my own life that I never sought after Him. Now that I am seeking an intimate relationship with Him, His hand is becoming more and more apparent in the everyday happenings of my life. I have learned that I have to dedicate time to Him just like any other relationship. My journey with Him is an everyday experience. He's never too busy to hear the cry of His child.

He's the only one that can bring about a lasting change in my heart. I seek Him in tough decisions and He's there for me no matter what. He doesn't try to control me, He's a true gentleman and He gives me free will. It's always my choice to follow His way or my way. But He also knows me perfectly. He knows the very thing that will bring me the most joy, satisfaction, and fulfillment in life. I'm in the process of being still and trusting in His will right now. It's difficult, but I'm learning.

This is a poem I wrote about my every day experience with God:

AN EVERY DAY EXPERIENCE

You gave me free will.
That's a great power,
A power that I can get lost in.
I did get lost.
I ignored my heart
And more importantly
I ignored Your will.

Lord, as I walk in life
I feel like a deserted city.
The people have gone.
Nothing is as it used to be.
So many doors have closed,
Many slammed in my face.
People I love have left my life
And all that remains is loneliness.

I searched for You,
I know You are the only one
Who can take this loneliness away.
Lord, as I walk in life,
I want to walk with You.
It's so easy to wander off,
But I long only for an every day experience with You.
Keep me from getting lost again.

It's always and everyday experience with you Lord.
You embrace my life with love and passion.
Please Lord, don't forget that I'm here.
Don't forget that my heart needs You.
It's an every day experience.

After so many years being in control of my life, I realized that I was so wrong. I was so far from where God wanted me to be. It wasn't until I surrendered the control of my life over to God that I came to the conclusion about Latin Lovers. Latin Lovers really do exist. They are those defined by the definition I just shared, not by the standards of this world. God is the foundation of their love and passion. They are men who persevere through hard times and trials to love and respect their families, friends, country, and their women too. They're not only passionate about sex, their passion saturates every area of their lives. In sharing my life with you, my hope is that you now have a greater understanding of my culture and that your perception of Latin Lovers now encompasses their true nature.

I listen to the relentless waves breaking on the shore with unharnessed power. They come in three second intervals and it's in that brief silence between that I enjoy the entire picture. The day I can finally say, "I've found *La esposa de mis sueños!*"

(the wife of my dreams!) My heart will be racing just because I'm in the same room with her. I will gaze into her eyes and get lost in a flood of images about our future together. We will become one flesh according to God's perfect will and we'll serve Him together. We'll build a family and a home and we'll grow old together. We will grow to experience the true depth of love such that we can say, "I love thee to the depth and breadth and height my soul can reach." Then, I will have finally become a true Latin Lover and I will be hers forever!

I want to take my time to breathe deep in life and appreciate every second. I know that the rest of my life will be anything but ordinary and I can't wait! But at the same time I know that life is fleeting and I don't

> "I love thee to the depth and breadth and height my soul can reach."
> Elizabeth Barrett Browning

want to miss anything. I want to soak everything in as it comes. The next story will in no way be the "Grand Finale," it will undoubtedly be the **"Great Beginning."** The beginning of one of the happiest of endings, the story of how I found that special someone I will be so happy to call MY WIFE!

Pero por el momento… FIN!

But for now…The End!

GREAT NEWS

I know I already said the end, but I couldn't forget the most important thing in my life—my relationship with the loving God through His son Jesus Christ. The great news is that the incredible intimacy I share with the King of the universe is available to all who will receive Him. You can walk through some simple, yet profound, truths with me right now and receive Jesus Christ as your personal savior. I invite you to make the greatest commitment of your life—one that will bring unspeakable joy, indescribable peace, and unimaginable hope. I promise it will be a decision you never regret.

> I know where I'll be when I die.
> **I'll be in Heaven** by the grace of God and
> the saving blood of **Jesus Christ**.

Many people are trying to reach God through their own efforts such as a good life, philosophy or religion, but they always fail. No matter how good you are or how many good deeds you do, you can't <u>earn</u> eternal life. It's a free gift! "For it is by grace you have been saved, through faith and this is not from yourselves, it is a gift from God – not by works so that no one can boast." (Ephesians 2:8-9)

God loves you and created you to know Him personally. Unfortunately, people are sinful, no matter how hard we try. We have free-will and have gone our own independent way and have broken that relationship with God.

Thankfully, "God showed His great love for us by sending Christ to die for us while we were still sinners." (Romans 5:8) Jesus is the <u>only</u> way back to God. Jesus said, "I am the way, the truth, and the life. No one comes to the Father except through Me." (John 14:6)

"Christ died for our sins...He was buried, and He was raised from the dead on the third day." (I Corinthians 15:3) Christ died to pay the penalty for our sin to bridge the gap that separates us from God.

| **Want to know how you can have that assurance too?** | **Read on!** |

| **It's simple really...** |

- You must recognize your need for Christ.
- You must confess your sins and ask for forgiveness.
- You must ask Christ to come into your life and make you what He wants you to be.

You can receive Christ right now by faith through prayer. Here's an example:

"Lord Jesus, I need You. Thank You for dying on the cross for my sins. I believe in You, and I open the door of my life and receive You as my savior and Lord. Thank You for forgiving me of my sins and giving me eternal life. Take control of my life and make me the kind of person You want me to be."

If you sincerely prayed this prayer today, rest assured that Jesus heard you and angels are rejoicing in Heaven!

Congratulations!

But, all is not done...

Accepting Jesus and dedicating the rest of our lives to Him does not make us perfect or prevent us from making mistakes in the future. Being a Christian is hard. We struggle daily with the sin and influences of this world. All is not a rose garden and I don't want to give you that impression, but it is an exciting and wonderfully rewarding journey!

> **The most important thing you can do is connect with a Christian who is able to help you learn more.**

Find someone by whatever means necessary…think back, do you have a friend that mentioned going to Church with them before? Return to the church you used to go to – they'd love to see you again!

No contacts? Walk right in any Bible-based church and see what they have to offer you. If you aren't thrilled with the first attempt, try another option or another church until you find a person who will spend time with you studying the Bible, answering your questions, etc.

Christian fellowship is very important.

Study the Bible and learn all that you can for the day when someone comes to <u>you</u> for the answers.

"Espero verte en el cielo"

(I hope to see you in Heaven!)

ISBN 1-41205080-4

769625

Made in the USA